NUMEROLOG

A Beginner's Guide to the Meaning of Numbers, Discover How Your Birthday and Date Affect Your Relationships, Yourself and Your Destiny

MELISSA GOMES
LITTLESPIRITUAL.COM

Melissa Gomes

https://smartpa.ge/MelissaGomes

Table of Contents

MELISSA
GOMES
LITTLESPIRITUAL.COM

FREEBIES

AND

RELATED PRODUCTS

WORKBOOKS
AUDIOBOOKS
FREE BOOKS
REVIEW COPIES

HERE

HTTPS://SMARTPA.GE/MELISSAGOMES

Freebies!

I have a **special treat for you**! You can access exclusive bonuses I created specifically for my readers at the following link! The link will redirect you to a webpage containing all my books and bonuses for each book. Just select the book you have purchased and check the bonuses!

>> https://smartpa.ge/MelissaGomes<<

OR scan the QR Code with your phone's camera

Bonus 1: Free Workbook - Value 12.95$

This **workbook** will guide you with **specific questions** and give you all the space you need to write down the answers. Taking time for **self-reflection** is extremely valuable, especially when looking to develop new skills and **learn** new concepts. I highly suggest you *grab this complimentary workbook for yourself,* as it will help you gain clarity on your goals. Some authors like to sell the workbook, but I think giving it away for free is the perfect way to say **"thank you" to my readers**.

Bonus 2: Free Book - Value 12.95$

Grab a **free short book** with **22+ Techniques for Meditation**. The book will introduce you to a range of meditation practices you can use to help you develop your inner awareness, inner calm, and overall sense of well-being. You will also learn how to begin a meditation practice that works for you regardless of your schedule. These meditation techniques work for everyone, regardless of age or fitness level. Check it out at the link below!

Bonus 3: Free audiobook - Value 14.95$

If you love listening to audiobooks on the go or would enjoy a narration as you read along, I have great news for you. You can download the audiobook version of *my books* for **FREE** just by signing up for a FREE 30-day trial! You can find the audio versions of my books (depending on availability) at the following link.

Join my Review Team!

Are you an avid reader looking to have more insights into spirituality? Do you want to get free books in exchange for an honest review? You can do so by joining my Review Team! You will get priority access to my books before they are released. You only need to follow me on Booksprout, and you will get notified every time a new Review Copy is available for my latest release!

For all the Freebies, visit the following link:

>> https://smartpa.ge/MelissaGomes<<

OR scan the QR Code with your phone's camera.

I'm here because of you

When you're supporting an independent author,
you're supporting a dream. Please leave
an honest review by scanning
the QR code below and clicking on the "Leave a Review" Button.

★★★★★

https://smartpa.ge/MelissaGomes

Chapter 1: Your Birthday Code

Numbers can help you strengthen your intuition. According to numerology, all numbers have esoteric meanings corresponding to your personality and destiny. So if you are wondering what number you are or why you feel so connected to certain numbers, you are in luck. This article will teach you how to use numerology to understand yourself better so you can determine your fate.

The root word of "numerology" is "number," of course. Numerology is the study of the occult meaning of numbers. It uses numbers to predict an individual's lifespan and personality arc. You can use the various mystical meanings attached to numbers with the mathematical properties of numbers to provide a deeper insight into a person's character.

The first very important number in numerology is a person's actual birthday. This is the actual amount a person was born with; these are the only numbers that can pertain to a person from birth to birth. A person's actual birthday is the most important numerology number because that number remains the same from lifetime to lifetime. However, the length of time a person stays alive is more significant than the individual's actual birthday.

The numerologists then calculate a person's soul age, the amount of time that has expired since the person was born. This number is calculated by subtracting a person's actual birthday from their total lifespan and is usually rounded off to the nearest year, and this can give you a clear idea of what path you should follow in life because it gives you hints as to what your destiny is.

To learn about someone's soul, look at the initial letter of their first name. The alphabet, used in numerology, is the numerologists' tool in calculating their inner meaning. Every number has a meaning and a unique vibration. You can use the vibration of any number to give insight into an individual's personality.

As each musical note produces a specific frequency that you may measure, numbers produce a specific frequency that can define a person's personality.

This book will reveal the wonder and magic in your codes, beginning with your Birth Code. The year you were born is very important because it greatly impacts your personality. The research shows that a person's personality changes from year to year. So you must understand how numerology calculates the numbers of your birth year so that you can properly interpret them. Your birth year shows the type of role you play in life. Also, you can use this calculation to predict your compatibility with others.

There are many other ways to interpret a person's future with numerology. One of the most common ways to do this is to create a birth chart by calculating how many positive numbers are present in your natal chart. This code can give you an insight into what your life will be like in the short, medium, and long term. It will also help you understand the codes of others.

Knowing your Spirit Blueprint and using your Birth Code may construct your world; this will support you in discovering your true inner destiny. Being aware of your Destiny and your compatibility with others may push you to find that perfect love or let you know if you need to work on yourself first.

When your soul's Birth Code and current cycles are synchronized, you naturally connect with abundance, and your well-being translates into riches of mind, body, and spirit. The numerology Birth Code of each individual shows the distinct ways they are intended to experience, explore, and manifest satisfaction and abundance.

Important Numbers on Your Birth Code

Your birth code has three significant numbers influencing your life. Your Birth Code has three unique numbers:

- **Your Birthday Number.** This is the day of the month when you were born.

- **Your Life Purpose Number.** This is the sum of your full birthdate.

- **Your Destiny Number.** This is the total number of letters in your name, as indicated in your birth certificate, as every letter is equivalent to a number. You will understand these details in the next chapter.

Your Birth Code reveals the mysteries of your birth promise and outlines how you think, feel, act, and live. Your Life Purpose Number interprets your soul's current mission so you can better understand where you are headed on your spiritual journey. You can discover the meaning of your life promises by analyzing your life purpose number.

Your Birthday Number

Even if you don't know someone's age, the Day of Birth number provides rapid insight into their natural demeanor, manner of being, and tendencies. The Birth Number reports on the natural inner rhythms of a person's life. To understand your Birthday Number, you first need to know the date you were born in the corresponding calendar year. If you were born with a double-digit number, add the two numbers together until you end up with a single-digit number called your root number.

For example, if you were born on the 29th, you can add 2 and 9, which becomes 11. Since you still have a double-digit number, continue adding the sum until you end with a single digit, in this case, 1 + 1, summing up to 2.

Your Life Purpose Number

Combining all three birth numbers provides your Life Purpose Number. This number will reveal who you are and how you may express your gifts, how you are currently using your abilities, and how your future may look if you use your natural talents to the fullest. Together with your Birthday Number and Destiny Number, the Life Purpose Number provides detailed insight into how you experience and express your life path. Your Life Purpose Number is assigned to you when you are born and does not change from lifetime to lifetime.

The Life Purpose number is calculated by combining all the single digits of a person's entire birthdate and then reducing that total to its single-digit "root" number. For example, if your birth date is May 20, 1981. Your birth month is converted to its numerical equivalent: 1 for January, 2 for February, and so on. The numerical birth date is now 5+2+0+1+9+8+1, which sums up to 26. Since you ended with a compound number, you will have to add them to get your root number, where your Life Purpose Number is 8.

A few exempted numbers are considered master numbers, like 11, 22, 33, 44, or others. If your birthdate sum ends with a master number, you can refer to another chapter that discusses this further.

Root Number Descriptions

Each single-digit number emanates a specific vibration, giving powerful qualities and vital energy to the individual who represents it.

1

If your Life Purpose Number adds up to 10, 19, 28, 37, or 46, one of your actual Birth Code numbers is 1. When you are energetically aligned, you are a natural and authentic leader, an original thinker, accomplished, active, energetic, strong-willed, innovative, driven, fearless, and creative; you work best alone, have unique ideas and methods, have firm opinions, and prefer time alone and seclusion. Number 1s tend to make good leaders and can also be argumentative. They are unique individuals who have original ways of seeing things.

1s often need lots of time alone to recharge their batteries and be happy and productive. Anything that is not natural will disturb them; this makes them prone to being dissatisfied in life and striving for perfection in everything they do. 1s thrive in work environments that do not allow much human interaction. They prefer to be in their inner world and reflect upon their ideas and plans. Practical people, 1s, have a hard time with abstract ideas and have a hard time visualizing how something will turn out. They tend not to want to count on people but themselves. They can get into trouble easily by trusting the wrong people.

2

Your Birthday Number is 2 if you were born on the second of any month. If your birthday is on the 11th, 20th, or 29th of any month, 2 is one of your essential Birth Code numbers. 2 is one of your key Birth Code numbers if your Life Purpose Number adds up to 11, 20, 29, 38, or 47. You are a peacemaker, a diplomat, imaginative, innovative, very sensitive, healing, have a well-developed intuition and an eye for detail, are helpful, supporting, kind, romantic, psychic: though you may keep it hidden, patient, cooperative, quiet, and loving when you are energetically matched. However, if you are not matched by energy, you may sometimes hide things or fail to recognize your emotional needs. As a peacemaker, you live for harmony and try to avoid conflicts at all costs; unfortunately, this can be harmful since your partner may always expect too much from you and always have difficulty saying no to something or someone. You may try to be someone you are not to please others or yourself. You want good relationships and people to trust and depend on you. You have strong intuitions and a wide imagination. You like to go by your feelings and avoid thinking and planning too much. Romantic and creative, you are good at working with your hands; when you focus on a project, you single-mindedly work until you are done.

3

Your Birthday Number is 3 if you were born on the third of any month. If your birthday falls on the 12th, 21st, or 30th of any month, 3 is one of your essential Birth Code numbers. If your Life Purpose Number adds up to 12, 21, 30, 39, or 48, 3 is one of your essential Birth Code numbers. When energetically connected, you are outspoken, artistic, independent, uplifting, fun, cheerful, passionate, funny, and creative.

You desire freedom of movement, speech, and writing, appreciate travel, are a lover of Truth, can readily detect a falsehood, and your smile brightens the room. However, if you are not balanced, you tend to be changeable, moody, superficial, vain, overly critical, and easily embarrassed. People often find you unpredictable and hard to trust. As a healer, you are helpful and compassionate; however, if you are not calm and centered or have not accepted your shadow side, there is a good chance you might become overly dependent or insecure. Grandiose, emotional, and sensitive, you can't bear hypocrisy or dishonesty and tend to dislike an entire group of people if they behave irrationally. You tend to hide your needs as a lover, parent, or friend.

4

If your birth date falls on the 4th, 22nd, or 31st, or your root number ends with a sum of 4 and your chakras are balanced, your Birth Code defines you as dependable, honest, practical, organized, disciplined, grounded, productive, loyal, patient, trustworthy and not scared of work. Those with the root number 4 are trustworthy and dependable. Out of balance, they can be inflexible, dogmatic, overly critical, and impersonal. Root Number 4 people tend to be fairly conservative and cautious and prefer to be financially independent. They may end up working too hard to take care of others. If you were born on the 4th, 13th, or 24th of any month, your Birth Code defines you as self-reliant, reliable, inner-directed, diplomatic, tactful, rational, workaholic and disciplined

5

Your root Number is 5 if you were born on the 5th of any month. If your birthday is on the 14th or 23rd of any month, or if your Life Purpose Number adds up to 14, 23, 32, or 41, you are an energetically aligned seeker of freedom, flexible, charming, a multi-tasker, humorous, adventurous, resilient, courageous, and versatile. You also have strong intelligence, appreciate change and mobility, travel frequently, are an excellent marketer, and have an active mind. Those under the number 5 are natural-born travelers and do well in fast-paced environments. However, if they are not energetically matched, they might be reckless, easily distracted, and have difficulty completing a task and staying focused on a single goal.

6

If you were born on the 6th, 15th, or 24th of the month, your Life Purpose number sums up to 15, 24, or 42; your root number is 6. You are caring, artistic, responsible, loving, creative, romantic, healing, committed to, and cherished by your family and friends, and you want harmony when you are energetically matched. Your natural gifts and abilities include encouragement, enthusiasm, and the ability to conquer your demons. You are also a born leader with a gift for organization and management. Suppose you are a 6 with a healthy relationship with yourself and others and are energetically matched; in that case, you are an amazing person to be around and are an important part of the community. You can be a control freak or too close-minded when out of balance. Your main challenge is learning to take responsibility for your past hurts and failures to heal and grow. To flourish and become your most authentic self, you must consciously choose to be at your best.

7

Your Birthday Number is 7 if you were born on the 7th, 16th, or 25th of any month. 7 is also one of your important Birth Code numbers if your Life Purpose Number adds up to 16, 25, 34, or 43. You are a seeker of freedom, adventurous, passionate, multi-tasker, compassionate, and thoughtful. You are spiritual or scientific, sensitive, dignified, smart, quiet, reserved, analytical, love to read, have distinct opinions about religion and politics, and like digging into the world's secrets when you are energetically linked. However, your body may become rigid and tense if you are not open or have not accepted your negative side. When this happens, you become inflexible and lack warmth. As a lover or parent, you may be bound by routine and find it hard to be spontaneous. Your challenge is to be more open to the unexpected.

8

You are energetically aligned if your birthday is on the 8th, 17th, or 26th of any month, or your Life Purpose Number adds up to 17, 26, 35, or 44. When you are energetically aligned, you are efficient, determined, abundant, a leader, ambitious, athletic, healthy, powerful, influential, visionary, reserved, responsible, strong, and disciplined. You manage your time carefully, have strong judgment, and succeed at activities that demand dedication, patience, and logical reasoning. You like freedom; you are honest, fair-minded, generous, enthusiastic, and compassionate. You are independent, self-confident, and self-reliant. You appreciate curiosity and learn by doing. Those with an 8 as their root number are known to be independent and have a personality that does not tolerate oppression. A seeker of freedom and new experiences, your innate gifts and abilities include leadership potential..

9

Your Day of Birth Number would be 9 if you were born on the 9th of any month. If your birthday is on the 18th or 27th of any month, or if your Life Purpose Number adds up to 18, 27, 36, or 45, 9 is one of your important Birth Code numbers. When you are energetically aligned, you are compassionate, wise, influential, artistic, magnetic, humanitarian, unconditionally loving, courageous, trusting, generous, creative, charitable, idealistic, and romantic. You can go to the heart of a problem and desire to make a difference in the world. Those with a 9 as their root number tend to be natural and spontaneous. As spiritual beings, their deep natural gifts include an ability to foresee the consequences of their actions.

Other Birth Code Numbers

You now understand how to compute two of your Three Important Birth Numbers, which you may use to read anyone easily. You also understand your Extended Birth Code Numbers and the life lessons they may hold for you.

You can also find your Birth Code through your birth name, which will be discussed further in the next chapters; this becomes a unique identifier for your soul and provides useful insight into who you are and your purpose here on Earth.

Chapter 2: Your Birth Name Code

There is no such thing as a good or bad birth number. Each digit in your Birth Code must be expressed positively; this means that 1 and 8 are positive energies, and 4 and 9 may be energies you need to work on. Only when the letters of your Birth Code have been expressed constructively can they affect you positively.

The third of your three primary birth numbers is your Destiny Number. It describes your profession, your life purpose, and your true Karmic path. This number is also expressed constructively as its sounds: Au, Vi, or Va for the Destiny Numbers 1, 5, and 9, respectively. Your Destiny Number also provides the keywords that explain your life purpose.

Once you have determined your primary purpose, look at the potential conflict that may be going on in your life according to the descriptions that the numbers represent.

Your Destiny Number is powerful and reveals your true path to happiness and prosperity. It is the energetic form of your Karmic Path. Everything in your life will lead you to that happy path, unfolding in the coming years. As you fulfill your destiny, you will reach your Karmic Dimension, the place of your highest inspiration and spiritual fulfillment. You will live in the golden light of happiness forever.

Calculating your Destiny Number

If you were adopted, use your birth certificate name from before you were six months old as your primary Destiny Number. For example, if you are 6 years old, you were 5 months old when you were adopted, you will have to use the name on your birth certificate from when you were 5 months old. If your birth name is not on that record, you will calculate your Destiny Number using the name on your adoption papers.

Each letter in the Pythagorean Numerology Alphabet system corresponds to a unique number. These numbers add to a root number that makes up your Destiny Number.

Add all the letters in the Pythagorean Numerology Alphabet that appear in your name, not including suffixes. Then refer to this chart below for the equivalent numbers for each alphabet. After computing each Destiny Number, you will see the Three Important Birth Numbers and a breakdown of how to blend the three numbers.

Description of Destiny Numbers

The Destiny Number reveals your unique purpose on this Earth. The Destiny Number represents your life path and your true spirit animal totem. Your Destiny Number is important, as it is the key to your primal purpose. It will point you to a place of deep spiritual fulfillment on your path toward enlightenment.

You were born without choice on your path in life, but through faith and positive thinking, you can overcome any obstacles. Once you have computed your Destiny Number from your birth name, here is a description of your Destiny Numbers.

1

You are an Innovative Leader when you are aligned with your One Destiny. You must be able to stand alone and explore new ideas without being interrupted. Eventually, your way becomes the way everyone finds the easiest to follow. You are a Universal Teacher when you are energetically aligned with your One Destiny. You deeply understand universal rhythms and enjoy teaching others the philosophies that influence you. You enjoy being the center of attention and surround yourself with people you admire while remaining a humble teacher at heart.

2

If your Destiny Number is 2, it is one of your important Birth Code numbers. You are a Master Caregiver when your energy field is in harmony with these Birth Codes. You must develop patience in your dealings with others and learn to understand rather than control others. When you heal yourself, you heal the world. As a Mediator of Peace, you may produce harmony and balance when energetically linked as a 2 Destiny. You are a natural healer, sent here to inspire and provide hope. Under Destiny Number 2, you can powerfully influence others and educate others about universal laws by helping others and showing others how to care.

3

If your Destiny Number adds up to 3, it is one of your important Birth Codes numbers. You are a Master Motivator when your energy field is in harmony with these numbers. You inspire others and can empower people with your artistic and communicative abilities. Feel completely happy about your professional projects. You have a true talent for teaching and inspiring others that brings you great satisfaction. Let your emotions flow and be as free of inhibitions as you can. Your openness will be contagious and inspire those around you to embrace their creativity. Those friends you meet through professional contacts will be long-term friends. As a Teacher of Wisdom, you may find great inspiration in philosophy and the arts and have a special talent for igniting the sparks of others' creativity. You express your creativity openly and exuberantly as an Expression of Joy.

4

When you are openly linked as a 4 Destiny, you must feel like your abilities are being used to build something practical, solid, and stable that serves a practical purpose. As a Dedicated Craftsman, you work on your projects steadily and without distraction. Fours are associated with practicality, so you must embrace the hard facts of any situation rather than the emotional content that may cause you to react out of turn. As you embrace your creativity, you find creative outlets in friends, hobbies, or travel. You experience life through your five senses, and you must take time to explore each sensation to its fullest. You are also highly aware of the outer magical world around you and seem to interpret the messages you receive from the spirit world. As a Master of Practicality, your goal should be to get everything done efficiently without being lax or careless.

5

When you have a 5 Destiny energy alignment, you desire to experience life fully, are naturally curious, and utilize your gift of communication to communicate messages that excite and liberate. When you think of yourself as a Dynamic Innovator, you naturally attract inventive and imaginative people interested in trying out new ideas with you. You represent newness in life and are optimistic about the future. Express yourself through your artistic abilities in a dynamic way. 5 is associated with personal freedom. When you open your alignment with this number, you express your freedom in many ways and must never question your intuition or beliefs.

6

You are optimistic and emotionally balanced when you have a 6 Destiny energy alignment. You tend to help others reach their dreams and aspirations, and you enjoy the excitement of change. Share your bright and energetic outlook with others. You encourage others to embrace change and rely on your dreams as a guide as you pursue your life purpose. You are a Healer of Love who inspires people to create something beautiful and meaningful when your 6 Destiny is energetically aligned. Your natural capacity for love makes others feel comfortable and safe around you. Your energy and intelligence attract new friends that allow you to share your talents and creativity. Partner with a compatible and equally creative person. As a Representative of Beauty, you may have a talent for bringing out the beauty in others.

7

When you have a 7 Destiny Number alignment, you are naturally intuitive, deeply sensitive, and desire to create beautiful things that inspire people and protect those in need. Sevens are associated with the visionary dreamer, so never lose faith in your dreams and visions. Create projects that are grounded in practical realities and have the potential to create practical value for all people. Express your creative talents with fine craftsmanship and detail. When you express your artistic energy, you draw people's attention, attracting them to your creativity and your natural ability to make others feel comfortable in your presence. As a dedicated Visionary, you naturally attract like-minded people inspired by your enthusiasm and optimistic outlook. Because you want to learn and search for wisdom, your greatest job setting allows you to find secrets and mysteries in science or spiritual disciplines.

8

When you are connected as an 8 Destiny, you must believe that you are capable of doing anything and use your innate daring, influence, and desire for success to realize your creative ambitions. Use your natural magnetic and powerful, stubborn side to your advantage and inspire others to believe they can achieve their creative goals. As a Representative of Power, you must use your energy wisely and strive toward accomplishment, success, and recognition. Your down-to-earth and highly rational approach to life attracts people who respect your opinions and your strong work ethic.

9

Your spiritual duty as an energetically linked Compassionate Humanitarian is to make the world a better place. Your energy field aligns with the number 9, and your curious personality naturally leads you to secrets and mysteries in life. As an Illuminated Helper, you inspire others to achieve their full potential and share that potential. Be a humanitarian who is always ready to help people in need and to help provide the resources necessary to inspire them to succeed.

You must commit your heart and soul to your work. Your quest for knowledge will lead you to many discoveries and joys. Because you are naturally sensitive, you are happy to be home and work alone when appropriate. Outwardly, you may appear reserved and introverted. Your flexible nature allows you to adapt creatively to critical situations. You can often make quick decisions and take action when others wait for more information. Your natural curiosity about the world draws you to scientific or spiritual mysteries. Your adventurous spirit lets you stretch the limits of what is possible and continually search for new success.

Chapter 3: Single Digits and the Three Pillars

The underlying energy of every number is symbolized by root numbers, which you might compare to the key of a piece of music. The structure of a musical composition is determined considerably by its key; the harmony will not sound good if it is carried out in another key. In the same way, your inner strivings and your outer activities resonate with the energy of certain numbers. They combine to generate visible and unseen code.

The numbers 1, 5, and 7 make up the Mind Pillar. Mind people appreciate learning and exploring new ground because they are analytical, cerebral, intuitive, ambitious, independent, humorous, and psychic. They are likely to be artistic and creative and are highly emotional. These people have a natural flexibility and tolerance for change.

The numbers 2, 4, and 6 make up the Manifestation Pillar. These individuals are patient and grounded, rely on order and discipline to achieve their goals, and have a substantial effect. They tend to be reliable and responsible people who are determined and confident. Manifestation enthusiasts must take the time to appreciate the manifestation process and examine their feelings before carrying out their ideas.

The 3-6-9 pillar makes up the Creation Pillar. Soul people value feelings more than the material world. They are spiritual, quiet, intuitive, sensitive, and sentimental. They make good listeners, yet they are independent thinkers and decision-makers. They are compassionate, caring, emotionally involved, creative, nurturing, energetic, friendly, and strongly desire to serve others. They need a place to chat, write, dance, and create in any manner they want. The 3-6-9 pillar guides the creative process.

In astrology, all aspects are reduced to 3, 6, or 9, the 24 hours a day add up to 6, and the 12 hours add up to 3.

Your three important Birth Number codes may be outstandingly successful. It may point in a certain direction in life's course that you are not yet willing to accept or are not emotionally prepared to go. To obtain a quick read on someone, use the three numerology pillars. They may assist you in understanding their outlook and natural approaches. The single-digit digits 1 through 9 have unique significance.

Single Digit Root Number Meanings

Consider which numerology pillar your three important Birth Code Numbers belong to. Identify if they are all part of the same pillar family or do they represent two of three pillars.

1

One denotes fresh beginnings, creativity, daring, excitement, and the desire to leave a distinct legacy. 1 individual rejects following the crowd and instead follows their urge to provide fresh experiences for others. A single person's mind is always buzzing with ideas, and they aspire to be the "star" in some fashion. They are unhappy with mediocrity and want to be important and influential.

The number one is dignified and forthright, with a keen sense of direction, and represents the masculine part of our human experience. Individuals under root number 1 expect respect, have strong opinions, appreciate solitude, and like spending time alone.

The number one is in the Mind Pillar, which suggests they have mental resources and an active imagination. They perform best when called upon and must avoid overanalyzing and stressing about the future. A 1 person can be stubborn, self-centered, and suffer from "bruised ego" syndrome. They can be boastful, aggressive, cynical, and egotistical and may even lash out aggressively to stop anyone they view as an unwelcome parental figure. Ones can be obstinate and inconsiderate of other people's feelings. Still, if they loosen the reins of control and use their good humor, they can instantly restore harmony and peace.

2

The root number 2 is the number of peace, communication, balance, and unity. It is connected to imagination and dreams, and 2 people are very sensitive, so be extra gentle with them. Twos are cautious and like to get approval from others before making a decision. They are easy to be with and have a magical touch of persuasion that allows them to get others to see things their way. 2s are naturally responsible, conscientious, efficient, and very psychic. They are generous friends, make great companions, and have a natural interest in the psychology of human nature. 2s are naturally very romantic, have a primal urge to please others, are secretive, and don't readily share their intimate thoughts, plans, or even what their next move will be. They are very giving with their resources and will usually attract financial well-being. Twos trust others implicitly and must learn to discern between what feels right and what feels just a little "off". A person under the root number 2 is sensitive, kind, and idealistic and loves to dream of bringing peace, love, and harmony to the world. You live in the shadow of your number and can be neurotic, touchy, nervous, and fear every kind of pain or loss.

Twos need a secure, loving home base and a harmonious environment to thrive. They need to accept that life is filled with both positive and negative situations and that they will sacrifice much to get their life back into harmony. 2s are shy and may freeze around strangers, but once they feel their heart engaged in a conversation, they open up the soft petals of their sweet, tender hearts to others. 2s are deeply affected by inconsiderate or rude behavior, but they will figure out how to justify such actions by others and forgive them. A 2 must learn to relax to regain and maintain inner harmony and peace. Deep breathing, exercise, and meditation are necessary daily.

3

A three personality is highly creative, action-oriented, and truthful and radiates with joy. They are curious, love to learn, and are the first number in the Creation Pillar and thus are fiercely independent, seeking total freedom of movement. 3s have a great sense of humor and a cheerful disposition and can see the bright side of any situation. They are also experts at comfortably mixing with any group and have a knack for adjusting quickly to different personalities or changing situations.

The 3 people are represented by two wide-open half circles facing the left, embracing everyone they meet. 3s are born to inspire, and their natural charm relaxes and disarms anyone with whom they make contact. 3s are driven by a deep ideal and will leave no stone unturned to find the truth. They are great detectives and can spot a lie in a second. They are also driven to succeed because of the pleasures it brings, not the position or power it brings. 3s thrive when they can travel, explore other countries, cultures, music, and people, and are deeply spiritual. They are charming, magnetic, and love to take risks, and they must have a sense of independence in any marriage union to feel the freedom that is integral to their happiness.

Threes can multitask, get distracted, and delay or dilute their divine mission's impact if they don't learn to focus and specialize in one direction at a time. They need to play and have fun, but they can also get lazy about practicing and developing their gifts. 3s can be wise and philosophical one moment and witty and funny the next but abdicate discipline and lack steady growth. They need to persevere steadfastly with their goals. To cure a negative emotional state or depression, just do it. Express yourself in any way you want to.

4

Four is a grounding frequency, a hands-on approach to life, and a mysterious quality connected to the divine. You are practical, trustworthy, and have a calm demeanor. The 4 vibration is organized and unpredictable. You love to go off the beaten path and explore your hunches and intuitive downloads but can be stubborn when making internal adjustments. The number 4 symbolizes the real reason for our life on Earth: We are divine beings of light having a human experience. The 4 people are grounded on Earth while exploring the wonderful gifts in the Pillar of Creation.

Four governs feng shui and helps you to stay balanced and healthy. Feng shui is the art of keeping your physical environment energetically clear and positive. As a 4, you love being part of a family and cherish your friends. You are tolerant and compassionate and mix with people of all means. When your energy is out of alignment, you may take a rigid approach to life, get stuck in a rut, become headstrong, and overwork. You may get too serious sometimes, forgetting to lighten up and go with the flow.

5

Five represents versatility, movement, decisions, risk, and a new beginning. It is also the midpoint of all three pillars and the middle of the Mind Pillar, which means you are naturally connected to higher consciousness. 5 governs groups or crowds of people, making you an adept social networker, performer, writer, or speaker. You enjoy big crowds and can sell ice to

Eskimos. The 5 vibration is very alert and bright and thrives when there is movement. You are an intrepid adventurer and enjoy travel, but tend to keep from emotionally engaging with ideas or people, which can lead to indifference about relationships. Under root number 5, you have a zest for life and a child's mind. You can rebound quickly from setbacks and move on with living.

Fives encompass the human experience, all five senses, and all contradictions. You thrive to experience, vibrate, and live to your fullest capacity and may fluctuate from feeling exalted to profoundly down for seemingly no reason. When the positive expression of the number 5 is not present, you may be critical of others and yourself and use your mind instead of your heart to find answers; this can lead to breakups and endings. You can be high-strung, have a nervous disposition, and crave change for the sake of change. Guard against impulsive actions and reactions, and learn to center your brilliant, magnificent gifts to maintain calm and peace.

6

As a person under root number 6, you are compassionate, loving, and responsible toward your family and friends. The number 6 represents nurturing others, being of loving service to others, being supportive, and being utterly devoted. You are highly magnetic and love to give affection and hugs, but you must learn to receive the bounty of love and luxuries life offers. Six governs human love and romance as well as money and abundance. You are in touch with exhibiting good manners and are tasteful, yet will not shy away from expressing yourself strongly when you feel passionate about something. You are artistic and love beautiful music, art, furniture, and clothing. You like to live in a sensually pleasing environment and love having your favorite colors and artwork in your home.

When you are a highly creative person who is attracted to abundance through your talents and abilities, you can use your voice to speak, teach, counsel others, share information, sing, or work in the healing arts or politics. When 6s is out of alignment, it can lead to a controlling and interfering nature, a domineering attitude towards others, and a tendency towards self-righteous behavior. A 6-person may want to follow the path of least resistance and may feel like they are being inconvenienced by choosing to commit to something; this can lead to indecision, laziness, and a tendency to magnify difficulties, which are often not even real.

7

Seven is a number of the spiritual seeker, the sensitive, mindful philosopher, and the brilliant analyzer. You love to learn, read books, and educate yourself, exhibiting a quest for gathering knowledge and gaining understanding. The number 7 has a horizontal line at the top, symbolizing heaven, and a diagonal line reaching below, symbolizing a bridging to the lower world. The number 7 is also a symbol of lightning, which can cause sudden profound shifts in a person's life. As a seven person, you are a seeker of wisdom, a natural researcher, and enjoy extended periods alone. You can be mysterious to others, as your quest for wisdom changed your early beliefs.

Seven is the final number in the 1-5-7 Mind Pillars and carries tremendous intelligence. You can be taken aback by the lack of understanding and intellectual capacities in others. You like to approach life from a logical perspective, yet eventually must merge intuition with logic to get to the deeper mysteries. You need privacy and a cave to escape to for solitude. You are loving and devoted, but don't expect your partner to live up to your long list of ideals. You thrive in nature and near the ocean, and you should take many getaways to refresh your heart, mind, and soul. Make your life a ceremony, a devoted song to Spirit, Source, or God. You are wise and naturally seek knowledge, but you can get impatient with those who cannot "catch on" fast enough. Also, you can get cynical about life due to unresolved emotions from previous life experiences. You are secretive and distrustful of others, but you must be emotionally vulnerable in relationships. A change of place or time in nature will help you reconnect.

8

The number 8 is the vibration of leadership, strength, abundance, financial security, and power. It is the number of entrepreneurs and the executive, and it is natural for an 8 person to experience obstacles and ups and downs, but they use these as stepping stones to success. 8 represents eternal life, making visions real, bringing them to Earth, materializing them into goods that can be exchanged for money, and representing the energy exchange of money. 8 people are often focused on money manifestation, whether they have it or not.

An 8 person is meant to lead in some capacity, is very realistic and organized, and has great organizational skills. They are also very warm and like to keep a certain image of themselves that is strong. The infinity symbol is also reflected in the balance of justice and honor that 8 people represent. They are ambitious and like to mix with dignitaries, but can feel lonely and need to be loved and cherished. Eights are only attracted to quality and will not buy secondhand clothes. They have the inner courage, the natural leadership, and the vision to achieve greatness.

An 8 out of alignment is egotistical, materialistic, and forceful and may not fully enjoy their journey. A person with destiny number 8 must pay attention to their heart and pursue happiness with the same wisdom, maturity, and discipline they devote to their divine mission. If you do not pay attention to your restless feelings, you might react with tremendous anger or exhibit a need for rest.

9

The number nine symbolizes evolution and an enhancement of psychic abilities and clairvoyance. A 9 person is warm, outgoing, and loving with a dramatic flair, compassionate, romantic, filled with unconditional love, kind, empathetic, patient, tolerant, and wise. As a 9, you have a powerful personality that you can use to manifest inspirational accomplishments and beneficial products or results. You are naturally very direct and expect the same from others, so you don't tend to play games to get what you want. The number 9 has a circle at the top, representing wisdom learned from the numbers 1 through 8 that preceded it. The number 9 is connected to Earth by a line on the right side, representing the artistic and creative side of the human experience.

The number 9 is the final number in the 3-6-9 Creation Pillars and represents a culmination and celebration of a mission accomplished. You are naturally honest and direct and keenly observe all energy around you. You may strive to be in control, but your independent streak may keep you from true intimacy. You approach life with passion and intensity and are noted for your generosity and enthusiasm. When you are energetically out of alignment, you hold onto resentments, become resentful of life, and can shut down emotionally.

Guard against being arrogant, unjust, or dishonest. Focus on creating beauty, love, and excellence rather than limitations, and your emotional touchiness will disappear naturally. When out of alignment, you can be stubborn, reacting with aggressive action and creating conflict. You need to learn to forgive and forget.

Chapter 4: Understanding the Master Numbers

Master Numbers have a higher level of responsibility than single-digit vibrations. To ascend to the higher calling of a Master Number, you must pay close attention to your inner calling, which will always reflect your soul's chosen path. Master Numbers also bring with them the refined energies of the vibrations that precede and increase until you reach the vibration of the Master Number itself. The Master Vibration adds to the qualities, powers, and energies of the Great Number vibration it precedes.

Master Number 11

When number 1 becomes number 11, it becomes the Psychic Master, bringing double new beginnings and enlightened leadership. The number 11 symbolizes the balance between the seen and unseen and must be brought into equilibrium; this can be accomplished by learning about yourself, what you value, and what you need. It pushes you to become the best you can be through your psychic wisdom and natural ability to reach out into the unseen world of spirit guides, guardian angels, and your Higher Self. The direct influence of Master Number 11 brings an enlightened sense of leadership, which inspires others to believe in themselves and to reach their full potential. The 11 influences you to be emotionally detached and rather objective in your approach to life. It provides opportunities to be creative, express oneself artistically, and do work that will enrich the lives of others.

The Number 11 represents an opportunity to express frustrations constructively. It is a number that asks you to master listening to your inner voice. Listen and understand both sides when you hear a sense of division, and then surrender to the light of wisdom within you. Master Number 11 is an inspirational spirituality number associated with the High Priestess. It encourages you to become one with your spiritual path and to courageously face challenges, obstacles, and darkness in your life.

11 is a master of combination and convergence of energies, ideas, and people. It merges the energies of 1 and 2, which combine to produce 3, the triangle. The ancient mystery temples had pillars on each side of the entrance. The pillars symbolized an initiation into the mysteries and miracles of life. The pillars were also a table for two and a seat for a third. The symbol of the triangle represents the masculine and feminine principles of life.

Master Number 11 offers you opportunities for creative expression and blending your wisdom with the collective wisdom of your group. It is asking you to let go of the past so that it may open you up to new opportunities to express yourself. This number has always been the role of a spiritual master. As an 11, you illuminate the truth and can channel negative or positive energy. You receive great inspiration through symbols, music, art, and sacred geometry. You can become an advocate for others, radiating confidence, dignity, and wisdom.

You must choose between endeavors that bring unity and endeavors that cause separation. If you don't explore your inner world, you will project your fantasies and neuroses on others instead and sabotage your goals. Remember that true success lies in inner life and harmony. The Universe created you as a lightworker to be of service to others and for their support of you.

A master's number requires high degrees of self-mastery. It is often lost in relationships and doesn't function well in group situations. Master Number 11 is about detachment, learning to let go, and flowing with the universal energies around you. You will lose touch with your needs if you work too hard for others, but you must seek a balance between support and service. You have a natural ability to help others open doors to their unique expression of the Universal Truth.

As an 11, you understand that the veil of illusion is lifted when we enter the 11 portal, revealing our true divine origin. The more you trust and surrender to your intuition, the higher your vibration. As your vibration grows, you move toward achieving balance in your life and can experience the eternal life force within you and, thus, be of service to others.

People under the Master Number 11 are about your divine purpose and soul mission. Your soul's purpose is to shine the light of awareness on humanity and to awaken their consciousness to the mystical essence of life.

Master Number 22

Number 22 is a Master Builder who brings positive energies of change, creativity, intellect, and learning to any area of your life. The creative energy of the 22 is inspirational and visionary. You are a builder of dreams and desires.

The Number 22 focuses on enhancing your knowledge, experience, and self-awareness. You are a teacher, counselor, advisor, and healer. The 22 is a social and intellectual number. It provides inspiration, guidance, and a separate way of looking at life. This master number calls forth your humanitarianism, kindness, and wisdom in life. 22 indicates expansion and growth through stable relationships. It is a positive vibration that is constructive in its energies and centered in its desire to serve humanity. It acts as a catalyst to awaken the mind to creative pursuits in art, music, or science.

The number 22 can indicate creative or harmonious energies depending upon the current placement of other numbers that precede or follow it. It can have either a positive or negative energy depending upon the circumstances you are experiencing. As a spiritual builder, the 22 creates structures that promote growth and harmony and offer life protection, security, and tranquility.

Master Number 22 requires tremendous inner strength, patience, and vigilance to stay "on track". Without consistent monitoring of your actions, you may get blinded by the negative actions of people around you, leading to delusion and frustration. 22 encourages you to be true to yourself and seek harmony in your environment and relationships. It wants you to trust your natural abilities and use your talents wisely to benefit humanity. It encourages you to express your thoughts and feelings clearly to help heal others and help them care for you when in need.

The essence of the creative 22 is to increase our opportunities in life by helping others and by helping them to help us. It helps us find solutions when things seem hopeless or give hope of a "new possibility". The number 22 encourages you to constructively use your intellect and be a positive thinker by nature. People with the 22 Master Number are most often unique individuals who are spiritual teachers or pioneers with a natural talent for influencing others. They strongly desire to use their knowledge and talents to help humanity. They are often teachers, counselors, advisors, or healers of some kind and use their intuition to provide insight and guidance to others.

The 22nd Number for the Master Builder brings change toward the positive and encourages self-expression through advancing our ideas or designs in modern life.

Master Number 33

Number 33 is the Master Wordsmith. It brings positive energies of inspiration, motivation, imagination, and wisdom to all areas of your life. This master number makes you share your wisdom and experience for the benefit of others. This Master Number focuses on your wisdom, compassion, and ability to manifest abundance in your life through positive thoughts and beliefs. The 33 is a friendly number that emphasizes positive interactions with others. The essence of the 33 master number is to encourage personal growth and development. It activates your intellect by providing you with opportunities to share your wisdom and inspire others to follow your example. The people who play important roles in your life are there to show you what not to do and inspire you to become a better person. Accepting all experiences and relationships as valid and useful in some way is the key to inner change.

Master Numbers are stepping stones to success, and the Architect of Peace Master Number uses its power to manifest great projects. The number 33 symbolizes unconditional love and sensitivity to other people's emotions. It accepts and loves anyone regardless of what they do or don't do. All that matters is that it cares about people and gives its love unconditionally. It represents communication and devotion to humanitarian causes. It also encourages you to have more compassion and understanding of the world in which we live. A great champion of world peace, the Architect of Peace Master Number constantly focuses on harmony with others.

The 33 Master Wordsmith is a master of words and wields them skillfully to achieve its objectives. This Master Number brings a balanced, peaceful nature and a strong sense of duty to your projects. It encourages balance and cooperation in relationships. The 33rd Wordsmith is a peacemaker who brings a peaceful approach to all situations and is an excellent negotiator and diplomat. It can help others resolve disputes and avoid conflicts.

The 33 is an architect of strong, stable structures with integrity and justice. The Master Wordsmith allows you to express yourself freely. It encourages and inspires other people to express themselves creatively. The 33 encourages the expression of love through the arts, music, or drama. The 33 is a master mason that encourages us to create structures in our life that support growth, harmony, and prosperity.

The repetitive number 33 is a code for someone who is creative and can be used to master art, music, and form. A Master Number 33 person takes on many responsibilities to activate the deep empathy of this powerful vibration, including experiencing great doubt, delusion, and disappointment. You may struggle with issues of intimacy and loyalty. On the other hand, you must learn to forgive others for not measuring up, beginning with yourself.

Master Number 44

As a 44, you are resourceful and have great mental abilities. You have great magnetism, leadership abilities, and powers of persistence and self-control. You inspire others by your ability to see goals and can project a vision before your associates to follow. You are a master planner in both business and personal life. This Master Number represents natural leadership qualities and a heightened sense of purpose and direction in your life. You are a visionary, creative thinker that can see the bigger picture in your life and around it. You strive for material success in life, but you also strive for mental and spiritual peace and tranquility.

Master Numbers are unique numbers that act as catalysts in helping you achieve higher success in your endeavors. You are a visionary who sees a bigger picture, can bring others along with you, and stay focused on that goal. In general, the 44 Master Planner brings powerful energies of innovative thinking and strong determination toward success. The 44 Master Planner shows stability to business and career opportunities and helps you get ahead in life.

You are a master planner who is in control of your actions. Your sense of direction is strong, and there is a special project or plan in your life that you naturally lead others towards.

You can inspire others with your problem-solving abilities. You are innately practical and strong and can bring together many different aspects of power and personalities to find seemingly magical solutions to problems others can't solve.

You are a Master Number 44 and are tirelessly engaged with your responsibilities and projects, reflecting the self-discipline and tenaciousness required for any great leader or organizer. You become inconsiderate, overworked, and overstressed when out of alignment. When out of balance, the 44 Master Planners can lose sight of the glamorous life they've imagined for themselves and must face the harsh reality of it. The number 44 encourages you to know your responsibilities, goals, and ambitions.

The number 44 can be the light in the darkness in a challenging situation, or it can inspire perseverance and endurance in a difficult time. It encourages spiritual development and stimulates your intuition. Through the 44 number code, you learn how to use the energy of this vibration to harmonize your mind and emotions to create positive change in every aspect of your life.

Master Number 55

The Master Number 55 symbolizes that you are a seeker of freedom and a brilliant intellect driven to explore and learn with increasing passion. You have unraveling lessons to learn in life as the complex number reinforces your need for freedom, independence, and self-expression. You should never mistake minor changes for fundamental shifts. You are a creative force on every level.

This Master Number brings a period of accelerating personal growth and change in your life. With the intensified experience and depth of understanding that comes from living with this number, you can appreciate life's gifts and grow spiritually. You have brilliant intuition and are highly conscious of your inner world and environment. You are an observer of your surroundings and aware of energies and vibrations around you.

A Master Number 55 person is creative, imaginative, and artistic. Master Number 55 encourages artists, musicians, and poets to excel at their creative arts. They have the potential to be leaders in any field but lack self-confidence and may become loners. They cannot fully commit to reaching their goals. They have difficulty relating to others and may experience feelings of isolation. On the other end of the spectrum, a Master Number 55 person is confident, adventurous, and driven toward success. With an abundance of knowledge and wisdom, they attract wealth and abundance.

Master Number 55 makes the person's purpose through their inner desire to express creativity. You are a philanthropist who is concerned with humanity's well-being and welfare. As a result, you may get involved in humanitarian causes and politics to help make the world a better place. You value freedom and convey a unique understanding of people's needs and spiritual nature.

Master Number 66

When your Destiny Number is 66, you are a cosmic parent who empowers others with your loving and supportive words and beautiful message. You have grace and compassion for yourself and others. You have strong spiritual healing abilities as a Master Number 66 person. You are a natural-born leader with tremendous insight into human nature and a passion for positively encouraging others through your words or your actions.

The 66 Master Number encourages you to notice and appreciate the subtleties in life. You have an innate ability to always see the good in others, and they sense your intentions are positive. You can bring people together through your master number energy to create a beautiful, harmonious community. Still, you may not realize your potential for leadership until later in life.

As a natural intuitive, you need to surrender to the subconscious realms to experience spiritual victory. Master Number 66 can awaken your potential and manifest your highest destiny in life. A Master Number 66 person is emotionally secure, sensitive, and compassionate. They exude confidence in their spiritual abilities. This Master Number bestows the power of understanding, awareness, and instinct. Number 66 is the number code of a generous person.

Master Number 77

The Master Number 77 is a "revolutionary" number that endows you with inventive genius and spiritual awakening. You are a natural leader with a charismatic presence that can inspire others with your vision and spiritual enlightenment. You can face a challenge with more than physical energy. You possess a special power and strength that compels others to follow your command. This cosmic number awakens the inner spiritual potential and desire for transcendence in life. It is a guiding light that leads you to your destiny and the realization of your spiritual mission in life.

As a spiritual icon, you are restless and seek freedom from the bounds of dogma. Your intelligence is multidimensional, complex, and brilliant. You quickly comprehend life's complexities and can easily navigate the ups and downs of change. You have a unique ability to function within any environment. You are a leader who can communicate well with others and gain their support and resources to implement your vision.

As spiritual teachers, you powerfully influence others with your positive outlook and wisdom. You hold a master number that resonates with a cosmic frequency of altruism and compassion for a more just and compassionate world. Your radiant energy and magnetic personality attract and inspire people to live healthy and fulfilled life. You can heal others spiritually, emotionally, and physically and encourage them to do the same in return.

If your Destiny Number is 77, you have double spiritual insight and psychic abilities. You are here to uplift and inspire many. You channel change in quite mystical ways, often unbeknownst to you.

Master Number 88

When your Destiny Number resonates with 88, you are a Master Executive who leads with a profound vision. Your vision will change the world and touch the souls around you. You are uniquely talented, with a keen sense of direction and purpose in life. The intuitive wisdom of your heart leads you on your spiritual journey and takes you to the highest heights. You can change the trajectory of human life on a large scale with your presence and wisdom.

Master Executive under the number 88 brings leadership qualities into your life. You are deeply intuitive and psychic, with the ability to feel and see beyond the realms of the five senses. You are a true visionary and master strategist who inspires others to reach beyond their current goals and surpass all expectations. You activate and focus your sense of purpose, energy, intelligence, and skill toward accomplishing your goals and dreams.

When the number 88 resonates in your vibration, you are immersed in a deep inner knowing and wisdom that reveals itself as you move through your life as a Master Executive. You possess remarkable talents that guide and support your life vision. By living your special number vibration, you apply yourself to the channel of pure energy that expresses through you. By being true to yourself, you deliver a special message to others about the truth of life and their potential.

As a Master Number 88 person, you are compelled by your spiritual calling to infuse the world with your wisdom, truth, and compassion.

Master Number 99

When your Destiny Number resonates with 99, your life embodies the qualities of Fulfillment through unconditional love. All answers and wisdom are contained within you. You are accomplished and have the answer for pretty much anything and know it. Your abilities can create fortunes in their own right. You are a super-conscientious person who sees clearly and sees the truth in any matter or situation.

The Master Number 99 is a cosmic number that is bestowed upon a truly divine person that illuminates your world with wisdom and truth, thus serving humanity. With the 99 Destiny Number, you are gifted with many abilities, including healing abilities, clairvoyance, and telepathy. You are one in a million with a unique sense of idealism, and I see you as a spiritual icon whose mission is to help others find their purpose and potential. As a person under the Master Number 99, you possess a vast amount of high vibrational energy and wisdom that resonates with 99, activating your natural abilities as you navigate your spiritual quest.

As a person governed by Master Number 99, you have a tremendous function for humankind and inspire others to reach their divine potential. You have a supreme mission to guide and protect the unfortunate and the lost in this world. You help raise the world's vibration by using your magnetic energy to inspire others to do their best. The Master Number 99 brings your life objectives into focus. You are destined to have a huge impact on the future, and you are destined to make a difference in the vibration of humanity's consciousness.

Chapter 5: The Non-Repetitive Double Digits 10-98

In this chapter, you will understand the non-repetitive double-digit numbers and how they relate to your inner energies. You already know how to calculate a single-digit number when reading a birthdate, and you can use this to understand how the present energies affect your life.

10-19

The number **10** is the vibration of instant manifestation, and the number 1 and 0 are the building blocks of sacred geometry and the universe. Dedicate your life to creating love and light, and you will manifest magical outcomes that will heal your work environments, relationships, finances, and health in this lifetime. You are highly creative and intuitive and strive to make the world a better place to live. You may need to give up something to achieve your goals.

The shadow side of number **12** is expressed when you feel like a victim, compromise your mission or values, or are bitter. You may have been emasculated or neglected in the past. The twelfth number vibration emanates openness, idealism, generosity, and service to others. You are part of the divine plan to help others. The twelfth person draws attention to two truths or viewpoints. It is helpful to know the masculine-feminine aspects of yourself and adapt to each situation.

As a **13**, you are a genius with an out-of-the-box approach to life. Through interaction with others, you have learned that manifestation is not about having all the right or perfect answers but taking action to touch someone positively. You have learned how to forgive yourself and others and to make amends for past transgressions. The shadow side of number 13 is expressed when you focus too much energy on the material at the expense of your spiritual nature.

The ancients associated the number **14** with the scribe, representing magnetic communication with the public. A great mind who has always learned and quickly grasped concepts and ideas. The application of life itself stimulates your mind. The number 14 vibrates with freedom, spontaneity, and universal love. The energy of the 14 numbers is healing energy, and service to others is second nature to you. Abundance comes easily to you. The shadow side of number 14 is expressed when you are out of alignment. Don't rely on others for advice, but turn to your intuition for making big decisions.

The number **15** is associated with family and harmonymagnetism, enchantment, and art. You are positively aligned with music, drama, and art and attract prosperity and people who help you with gifts and favors. You are a charismatic entertainer—a well-known personality or influencer within your community. You like to be recognized for greatness and strive to be the best at your work. The shadow side of number 15 is expressed when you are out of alignment. You may step on people's toes or be overly curious.

The number **16** involves abundance and prosperity. As a master builder, you use determination and foresight to accomplish your goals. You are compassionate when faced with adversity. Seeing the bigger picture and learning from experience help you plan for the future. Sixteens are a powerful number of spiritual transformation and the number of listening to your inner voice.

You should never ignore your intuition, as ignoring them can attract challenges. When you are out of alignment, the shadow side of number 16 is expressed through promiscuity, unfaithfulness, impatience, overanalyzing, and being impulsive or reckless.

The number **17** relates to being a spiritual number and represents the Star of the Magi. People with this number in their soul Blueprint often overcome challenges and can align to love and peace. People with number 17 characteristics may act as peacemakers, healers, or artists. Your optimistic attitude encourages those around you. 17s can care for others but need to learn to be open-hearted. The number 17 opens the door to the Universe for you. Self-expression and spirituality go together with this number. The shadow side of number 17 is expressed when you can't follow your dreams or feel lost on your journey through life.

People with the number **18** in their numerology love to dream and require more time to rest for their amazing imagination to become conscious. It represents good luck and success.

You can move mountains and build empires. You like watching others work and can easily implement their dreams or demonstrate a way to achieve their goals. You naturally attract people who need your help or support. The number 18 connects with the principles of life to unleash your creativity, the Kama Sutra to seduce others, and the supernatural intuition of spirit guides and angels to guide you to higher consciousness.

The ancients called **19** the "Prince of Heaven," which represents a vibration of initiation. You may have to start from scratch. The number 19 is associated with confidence, courage, and new beginnings. You are a natural-born leader with the mindset to push the envelope in new directions. You long to travel and explore new ideas. You are a pioneer for new ideas in physical reality. Your courage is outstanding, but your attitude is not always stable or grounded. The shadow side of number 19 is expressed when you are out of alignment. When number 19 is out of alignment, you feel insecure, lack confidence, get impulsive, and may turn to deceit.

20-29

The double-digit number **20** is called "The Awakening" by the ancient Chaldean priests. You may succeed in life as part of a team, and you must constantly adapt and renew your life. 20 is associated with true love, compassion, and gratitude. This number demonstrates how you can lead others through inspiration and motivation. The number 20 brings together the principles of life to unleash your creativity and the supernatural intuition of spirit guides and angels to guide you to higher consciousness. The shadow side of number 20 is expressed when you are out of alignment. You may be drawn to supreme power and compromise your values and morals to gain it.

The number **21** is the mystical number of cosmic consciousness, and the truth shall set you free. You are highly creative, versatile, and well-rounded and can express yourself through any modality, career, form, or material. You are more spiritually advanced than a 19 or 20 and understand the underlying aspects of creation and soul. The shadow side of number 21 is expressed when you are out of alignment. You may get lost in spirituality or become selfish.

The **23** is the number of life and represents the desire for freedom and enjoyment of life. You have a quick mind and a great memory and learn easily. You have a magnetic presence and powers of suggestion, attracting abundance and nurturing relationships. You love your home, children, and nature and take responsibility for your life and goals.

Those under the number **24** are loyal and committed to the ones you love. You are a thinker and idealist who needs quiet time and tends to be more reserved. You can be a spiritual crusader and learn from past mistakes. When 24 is out of alignment, you may ignore your needs, become a workaholic, or feel that others are dominating you. You may be overly bossy or show resistance to authority.

The number **25** denotes new beginnings and second chances. It represents "grace upon grace", forgiveness, diplomacy, introspection, sensitivity, curiosity and ideas of intuition.

You recently discovered your spiritual purpose or feel that you have reached fulfillment in your life. You can see events from above and handle business from a position of wisdom. You may have been through painful experiences in life, but your desire to do work is stronger than your fear of failure. The shadow side of number 25 is expressed when you are out of alignment. You may be obsessed with perfection and lose touch with your inner self.

People with the number **26** in their charts have the most energy in their soul Blueprint and represent love and idealism. You are gifted with natural leadership and are excellent in the business, money matters, and management. You understand the material/physical world and intuitively know what makes virtually any enterprise work.

Twenty-seven is a number that symbolizes courage, love, compassion, and wise leadership. You love to share and uplift without expecting anything in return. You have a passion and deep knowledge of your spiritual self. The shadow side of twenty-sevens manifests when you don't listen to your inner voice or are too influenced by society's trends.

As a **28**, you have an original approach to life and want to explore life to the fullest. You are here to remind others of their eternal connection to the soul. You have excellent powers of concentration; your powers of vision allow you to see the future in rich detail. 28s can be pessimistic when unbalanced, have unrealistic expectations of others, and are pessimistic about love.

When taking relation to a **29**, you are highly intuitive, have faith in your gifts, and trust in the goodness of your soul. You take your life and role seriously and demand much from yourself. You follow your intuition and perfect your talents. 29s strongly desire to succeed and master the art of making dreams come true.

30-39

Those individuals with **30** in their number are achievers in all aspects of life. You have confidence and are goal-oriented. Thirty is a reflective number that proves you are capable of self-renewal and creative change. 30 is here to uplift, share the optimistic side of life, and celebrate. You possess the ability to motivate others to succeed. The shadow side of number 30 is expressed when you are out of balance. You may be overly negative but always in control, or you may be too critical and judgmental.

Thirty-one people can be realists, natural-born negotiators, and great businessmen/women. As a 31, you are realistic about the world and can particularly solve problems. You have a strong will to achieve your goals and make a positive impression. The number 31 signifies genius and out-of-the-box thinking. You need time alone to make your ideas and thoughtful approaches real and have a great desire for security, though not at the expense of personal freedom.

The number **32** is about freedom and connection to people and is expressed through magnetic presence or speech. You are like a warrior, activating your sense of responsibility and what is for everyone's highest good.

34 governs order, steady growth, and a patient approach to manifesting your goals. You are a quick thinker, an excellent planner, and have a logical approach to life's challenges. You believe in an innate power within all things and believe in fortune favoring the prepared.

The **35**th number's energy exchange of money fascinates you, and you are generous, affectionate, charming, and fully engaged in your independence. You have naturally large energy reserves but can be judgmental and self-indulgent.

As a **36**, you are here to live in alignment with your heart center, and you must use the energy living in your inspirations and inventions for good. When you are out of alignment, you may experience cycles of ups and downs, act in haste, or be emotionally distant.

Being in number **37**, you are sensitive, private, and love to have good friendships. You are also good with the public and are deeply spiritual. A 37 has a strong sense of self-worth and needs support. You are charitable, compassionate, and concerned about the needs of others.

38s are about making a successful career transition and responding to sudden changes. When you understand your passion and desire, you succeed in your personal and professional life. This number denotes natural clairvoyance, spiritual leadership, and entrepreneurship, and the shadow side of number 38 is expressed when you are out of alignment.

Number 39 symbolizes enormous strength and will power. It symbolizes growth and ability to synthesize knowledge into power.

40-49

The number **40** means that you are dedicated to following a strategy or plan of action and are a natural peace maker. You are a born leader who desires to keep peace in the hearts and minds of others. On the downside, it is expressed when you are out of alignment.

In number **41**, you are open, flexible, and quickly bounce back from challenges. A 41 is conscientious and has a great sense of responsibility to others. You are gifted with foresight and are a natural problem solver. The shadow side of forty-one is expressed when you are out of balance. You may be paranoid, worry excessively, or be indecisive.

42 governs affection, giving, and receiving; your home environment must feel beautiful and exude warmth. You have an innate ability to solve conflicts and want to be of service to others. As a 42, you are self-sufficient but need to connect with others and recognize the depth of love that exists everywhere.

43 symbolizes a strong intuition, and you are practical, creative, and strong in both the physical and spiritual realms. 43s respond well to protection and have a strong appreciation for nature to ground them. You have a strong, energetic center that needs to be nurtured and fed.

Number **45** gives you magnetic energy, the ability to communicate and experience the freedom of movement, and the wisdom and love of all the previous eight single-digit numbers. Family dynamics influence the shadow side of number 45 or people who may have issues with abandonment and jealousy.

46 owns the ability to initiate change and travel accordingly. You are heart-centered and show great love, compassion, and generosity. In number 47, you project magnetic and charming energy. You are an ambassador to other realms, operating simultaneously in both worlds and dimensions. You possess the ability to experience greater depths of love, and you are a natural teacher.

Number **47** is the number that completes all eight single-digit numbers and represents the maturity of knowledge and experience. You aim to capture the world around you and have great respect for human life and Mother Earth. The shadow side of number 47 is influenced by greed, lack of self-confidence, and follow-through.

In number **48**, you are deeply sensitive and spiritual. You are a dreamer, a magician, and also very wise. You have a strong sense of empathy and compassion for others. The shadow side of this number involves self-sacrifice and an inability to accept yourself and your life path lovingly.

As a **49**, you have compassion, brilliant ideas, and integrity that will benefit many. You are loyal and affectionate and are naturally patient and honest. However, you are also vulnerable to other people's perceptions that you lack flexibility and are a difficult person to be around when you are negative or gloomy.

50-59

As a **50**, your magnetism is strong, quick-witted, innovative, and very strong-willed. 5 blends your quest for freedom and joy with the 0 of divine protection. You may be drawn to serve in a public way or use your eloquence in public speaking.

The ancients referred to **51** as the "Warrior" number. You are an innovator and visionary to the highest degree, filled with helpful ideas, and have an active mind. When the number 51 is out of alignment, you can be cruel to others or harsh on yourself.

The number **52** is a powerful vibration that brings an enormous appetite to learn mystical secrets and explore the unknown. You are deeply committed to your cause but may manifest this through shyness or fear rather than having the courage of your convictions.

53 is a leadership number, and you are oriented towards financial abundance and business. It governs the gift of giving, generosity, and human service. You are very sensitive and intuitive, and you have access to unseen worlds. When number 53 is out of alignment, you can be doubtful or indecisive and hesitate in your actions.

Number **54** means you are humanitarian, compassionate, righteous, and a natural leader. You enjoy helping humanity and desire peace on Earth; this includes a benevolent royal family and a successful leadership base. You have an independent streak but need to be nurtured and loved.

56 is a highly sensitive number; you are charming, popular, loyal, and affectionate. You have great insight into other people and situations and are very diplomatic in communications. The dark side of number 56 is indulgent and selfish.

In number **57**, you seek power and leadership and succeed when your intentions are clear. Success comes to you in many forms, from leadership to wealth. You have an inner strength that is capable of withstanding great stress. This number also stands for social influence. You may lack confidence and experience mood swings when your energies are out of balance.

As a number **58**, a vibration of peace and balance, you are very loving and have a natural talent for communication. You have natural empathy and compassion for others. A 58 is also spiritually inclined and empathic, with a strong desire to help humanity by healing broken hearts. The shadow side of number 58 is expressing when you lack confidence, delay projects, or desire conflict with others.

As a **59**, you are persuasive and brilliant in how you connect through the heart and the mind. You thrive in diversity. 59s are passionate about life and constantly seek to expand their minds through reading and study. When you are out of alignment with number 59, you may risk too much just to feel alive.

60-69

The number **60** relates to love, service, compassion, harmony, joy, gratitude, warmth, and pleasure. You are charming, magnetic, wise, artistic, and responsible. 60 means you are a spiritual being expressed as a human being. You nurture others and deeply appreciate the beauty in nature and the arts. As a 60, your ability to serve and inspire others is highly developed; you are a natural healer and spiritual guide.

61 is a number related to intellectuals and idealists. You have a strong interest in mysterious, strange phenomena and divination arts. You are also good at keeping secrets. Number 61 can make you feel uncertain and hold you back. Tap into discipline and self-confidence to move forward.

62 comprises 6 and 2 and makes you a wonderful caregiver, healer, and mentor. You are also focused on manifesting financial abundance. Both people will appreciate your kind and gentle nature. The shadow side of number 62 is self-doubt.

63 is a highly passionate and creative number. You have a deep desire to uplift the world and create something of value for others. The unbalanced number 63 is expressed when you are out of alignment. Guard against hopelessness and self-consciousness.

As a **64**, you are highly intuitive and have fantastic communication skills that connect you with others instantly. You can achieve great success through teaching. 64s willing to do whatever it takes to succeed, a born leader. When out of balance, you may resort to fear and identify with suffering when out of balance.

Number **65** asks you to balance freedom with family commitments and to handle money matters with wisdom and care. You must be self-supporting, do your work, and have financial security.

67 is an energy power number and denotes powerful spiritual and mental adeptness. While 67s possess a magnetic personality and wonderful creativity, you sometimes drift into illusion and fantasy. 67 gives you sensitivity, empathy, and compassion for others when in balance.

68 is a great number for proclaiming your message and connecting with others. You enjoy making good, uplifting choices and have a sense of humor. A 68 is also highly investigative, highly intelligent, and has a strong psychic ability. On the other hand, when out of balance, you risk feeling powerless. You also realize deeper insecurity, self-doubts, and desires for material security keep you from realizing your true potential.

69 activates deep, profound loving kindness and responsibility to others, and you want to nurture or teach in some capacity.

69ers are extremely loyal and devoted to their families, friends, and partners.

70-79

The number **70** vibrates the forces of life, creation, and balance. As a 70, your sense of self-worth comes not from material wealth or success but from knowing that compassion, gentleness, patience, and faithfulness are the basis of a balanced life. You possess great wisdom, courage, strength, compassion, vitality, generosity, determination, and loyalty.

71 is a spiritually powerful number possessing extraordinary intuitive abilities and excellent for manifesting material well. You are an eccentric and a natural loner who needs to spend time in a place of serenity. You are highly intuitive and seek to learn the truth.

72 is the number of compassion and artistry, and you are highly skilled at handling wealth and completing major projects. When out of alignment, 72s can enter a trap of empty materialism and are attached to other people's money.

73 is among the most spiritual numbers with healing and other psychic abilities. As a 73, you can make it through life's difficulties with grace and wisdom. The lesson of 73 is forgiveness, understanding, compassion, and humility. Your compassionate nature is, however, hidden deeply by fear or insecurity. You radiate trust and respect; you live with integrity and dignity when in balance.

The number **74** carries a highly romantic nature. You are psychic and can channel energy. Peace to the number 74 is to be found within oneself and expressed in relationships. In troubling times, people relating to this number feel adrift and helpless and withhold their power.

75 is the most positive number related to finances, prosperity, and material needs. 75 possesses a refined and honest business sense and the ability to offer helpful counsel to friends and clients. 76 signifies one's opportunity for self-mastery and abundance through acquiring knowledge.

You are aligned with the **76** vibrations and enjoy working steadily and for long hours. You embrace change and transformation. When out of balance, you can become impatient and harsh. You may also discourage others by being overly critical of their ideas or actions.

78 stands for wealth, alchemy, and fulfillment. You are magnetic and easy to relate to on many levels. Your ability to focus and concentrate allows you to work effectively with others. 78s with high ideals and ideals can put a lot of pressure on themselves and others to fulfill expectations of perfection.

When **79** is your Master Number, you receive the expansiveness of 1 and the enlightenment of 9. You are bold and confident and have the mastery necessary to lead others. People are drawn to your charisma and ability to uplift others. The shadow side of 79 includes self-sacrifice, which may be motivated by concern about others, a desire for harmony, or a need to avoid conflict.

80-89

80 is a number that executive leadership and business relate to. You are good at holding a vision and leading others, and you will focus your mind on attracting prosperity. When out of balance, 80 becomes obsessive with money, success, and away from family and friends.

The number **81** gives you wisdom and power and the ability to help others let go of their emotional blocks and guide them into a place of self-confidence and creativity. When in balance, you are confident, honest, and sincere. When out of balance, you become controlling and rude or deceitful.

82 is the number that shows leadership and balance. You are kind and gentle, yet strong and confident. You vibrate with spiritual knowledge and understanding. You possess the ability to connect with others on a deep level. As a number 82, you are determined and have strong inner willpower. When out of balance, you might become rigid and intolerant of others' opinions and attitudes to life.

83 is a highly intuitive vibration that allows you to bring the unseen into conscious awareness, making you feel strong and confident. When you relate to others from a centered place of love, your energy is magnified, and your power is increased. Eighty-three may come across as being aloof, detached, or mysterious. When out of balance, you may be apathetic.

84 is a number that focuses on leadership and spiritual awakening. You are magnetic and intuitive and possess great visualization powers. The number 84 often carries a healing talent and a strong desire to heal the emotional wounds of others as well as manifest financial abundance. When out of balance, you risk feeling alienated and alone.

85 enjoys hard labor as long as it can incorporate freedom and vision. It needs to balance pleasure and work. 85 consists of a strong desire for success and accomplishment in all areas of life and can use success as a yardstick for self-worth. When you feel selfish and self-centered, others are turned off by your energy.

People under compound number **86** are fantastic for networking and communication. You enjoy working with other people and like to teach or help others. 86s possess great physical vitality and high intellect. You are sensitive to others' needs and can be overly involved in pursuits that lack inner meaning. When out of balance, you may lack sensitivity and trust in others.

87 brings leadership to a level of magic and allows you to facilitate a spiritual awakening in others. You thrive in a secure, loving home base that provides freedom for adventure. You are available to others in your relationships, yet not easily hurt. You radiate self-confidence, intelligence, and self-control.

The number **89** means effortless success and material rewards. Others easily recognize you for your cheerful personality, quick wit, and ability to communicate clearly and effectively. 89s come across as positive and encouraging. You may be naive and gullible and risk being exploited by others.

90-99

90 is a wise leader who brings a strong commitment to inspiring others. This compound number makes you naturally intuitive and psychic and possess great wisdom. Your life purpose involves revealing higher truths to those you encounter. When out of balance, you can become isolated or caught up in debates or arguments with others.

The number **91** combines endings and beginnings and brings tremendous manifestation abilities. As a master number 91, you have the potential to achieve much and touch many lives. You emanate happiness and harmony, yet fear the vulnerability that authentic attachment can bring.

92 is a highly intuitive number that takes life and role seriously. You balance love and intimacy, compassion and cooperation, and have a major mission to help humanity. Number 92 can represent division and indecision. You may trust too easily and get anxious around others.

As a **93**, you are highly intuitive, need outlets to express your feelings, and love to learn. You can tap into your mind and heart, giving you an easy grasp of the matters. The shadow side of number 93 is expressed when you are out of alignment and may have difficulty committing to projects or partnerships.

94 creates a strong urge to manifest wisdom and love. You have an affinity with group activities and are good at inspiring others to seek their higher purpose in life. Ninety-four combines deeply felt spiritual impulses with a sense of understanding and empathy. You are likely to be misunderstood by others.

As a **95**, you embody freedom from a soulful place of compassion, and you love movement and travel. You are a force to be reckoned with and can bypass most structural challenges. 95s lead with their heart rather than their head and need time to themselves to recharge their batteries.

96 is a powerful vibration of unconditional love, compassion, and alchemy. You are highly artistic and very creative, imbuing magical vibrations in every heart you touch. You may be easily influenced by others and lose control of your emotions.

97 is a vibration of royalty that needs peace to channel wisdom. These people can attain great heights in this incarnation. Important spiritual machinery is in place with this number. When you feel out of balance, the number 97 may mean you are disinterested or feel insignificant.

98 is a very romantic vibration and represents leadership through love and inspiration. If in balance, you have integrity, depth, discipline, and an idealism rare in many leaders. You can help others fulfill their dreams. However, you may become highly sensitive, have difficulty sharing your true feelings, and come across as aloof.

Chapter 6: The Numbers Behind your Name Letters

The alphabet conveys sacred symbolism and can be used to access another part of a person's soul contract. Pay attention to the meaning of each letter and the words that begin with that letter in capitals for even more insights.

Letter-Number Conversion Table

1	2	3	4	5	6	7	8	9
A	B	C	D	E	F	G	H	I
J	K	L	M	N	O	P	Q	R
S	T	U	V	W	X	Y	Z	

A

The letter A is the first letter of the alphabet and represents air; this represents the Alpha and the Omega, known as the first and last. This letter takes people back to the beginning, connecting them with their soul mates. The letter A equates to the number 1, where creation occurs in physical form. When A is in a person's name, it means they are ready to manifest their soul mate or a life partner.

A is the beginning and is nine times more masculine than feminine. It represents the first spirit to evoke change, no matter how subtle. Reception of A is the act of acceptance. Receiving the letter A means you are ready for a soul mate, and the receiving individual is now ready to summon their soul mate's presence within. The coming together of energies can spark transformation caused by new ideas, creativity, and communication.

B

The letter B is made up of a straight line and two curves and shows that you can handle more than one activity at a time. The letter B is for the balanced energies of yin and yang, represented by the symbol for balance, the Tao or Taijitu symbol, which is composed of two interlocking black and white circles.

The letter B is made up of straight lines and curves and is masculine nine times more than feminine. The letter B is associated with football, baseball, basketball, and hockey and stands for ambition, dominance, and control. When the letter B appears at the beginning of a name, it means the individual is in good health. The person may be athletic or ambitious and is generally quite attractive.

C

The letter C is made up of straight lines and one curved line. C stands for change and being analytical as well as creative at the same time. The letter C is ten times more masculine than feminine and is associated with clay and terracotta sculptures.

When the letter C appears in a person's first name, it means the person is filled with creativity. The person tends to be calm and analytical and may have inherited artistic talents from their mother or father. The letter C is also a symbol of endurance, and endurance symbolizes perseverance, the ability to pursue a goal with continual effort and action even when times get tough.

D

The letter D comprises straight lines and two curves representing yin and yang. The letter D represents death and rebirth. Containing the combination of yin and yang, the letter D represents the doorway between two worlds. The letter D carries the power of sacrifice, creative energy, violence, healing, heightened awareness, healing, and crisis management and is balanced by the letter F.

When the letter D appears in a person's first name, it represents a person with an openness toward spirituality and the occult. The person can see both sides of a story and navigate turbulent energies with grace. People with the name D can achieve physical perfection through hard work and dedication.

E

The letter E is made up of straight lines and one curve and represents new beginnings and earth energy. The letter E represents growth, ego, and marriage. E is the fifth letter of the alphabet and means the words "east" and "east" in another language. E represents the number three, the creation, and the mother's womb. The number three signifies the three main principles of the universe; creation, regeneration, and destruction.

When the letter E is spelled in a person's name, it signifies a person born in the East. The person may be spiritual and aligned with the earth, or the element earth is their soul essence. People who bear the name E tend to be nurturing and may be gentle or sensitive.

F

The letter F is formed as a curved shape with two straight lines and represents water energy. The letter F means "father" and "father" in another language and symbolizes power and strength. F is approximately nine times more feminine than masculine. The f represents femininity and fertility and is associated with the moon, femininity, the womb, intuition, and fertility.

When the letter F is included in a person's name, it symbolizes a person dedicated and loving to family. The person may possess certain traits that come from a bloodline, such as the trait of empathy or the ability to be intuitive and compassionate toward others.

G

The letter G is made up of two straight lines and one curved line, representing fire energy. The letter G represents the spirit of God. It is five times more masculine than feminine. G is the seventh letter of the alphabet and means the word "gold" in another language. G represents the earth element in the tarot card, the 8 Coins.

When the letter G is found in a person's name, it signifies a well-grounded person. The letter G represents the eight pillars of protection in the tarot card, Strength, which denote stability. As the earth element, the letter G represents being connected to the earth, to nature. It also represents a time of change, action, and new beginnings.

H

H is made up of two vertical lines and one horizontal line and can see clearly in any direction. H is the eighth letter of the alphabet and stands for the word "home." H represents the height of spiritual consciousness and spiritual awakening. It stands for the sun god Helios.

When the letter H is a person's initial letter, it symbolizes a person who is a born leader. The letter H represents the cards of the Major Arcana, the High Priestess, which ties back to the energy of the word "home." The High Priestess also represents the cycles and cycles of life. Having the H in a person's first name symbolizes someone who is humanitarian.

I

The letter I is a three-line shape representing air energy. The I represents words that start with the letter I. The I is the ninth letter of the alphabet and means the words "ice" and "ice" in another language.

The letter I appear in a person's name signifies a person well grounded in life. A person with the name I strive for success in life but is equally comfortable with the pursuit of knowledge.

J

The letter J is made up of two curved lines, representing water energy. The letter J is the tenth letter of the alphabet and stands for the word "just." J represents calmness, balance, patience, love, and financial success. This letter also represents the root number 1, which signifies leadership and the qualities of independence, strength, and integrity.

The letter J in a person's first name signifies a person's ability to be detached from a situation and see the bigger picture. A person bearing the name J is considered a strong leader but may have a penchant for being a perfectionist.

K

The letter K is a single straight line representing the element of fire. The letter K represents the words "king" and "king" in another language. K is the eleventh letter of the alphabet and means the words " cook" and "cook" in another language. The letter K also signifies the root number 2, that of duality.

The letter K in a person's first name signifies a person whose life is influenced by money, wealth, and abundance. The person may study hard to get a good job, earn money and pursue higher education to achieve material success and stability. The person has often been taught to follow the rules.

L

The letter L is made up of two curved lines representing the element of water. L represents words that start with the letter L, like the color light pink and the word beautiful. This letter signifies the number 3, where things tend to come in pairs and balance each other out.

When the letter L appears in your name, it symbolizes that you are an intuitive person. The letter L is often associated with femininity and fertility. L is the twelfth letter of the alphabet and stands for the word "level. " L represents the element of water in tarot.

M

The letter M is pronounced with closed lips, representing silence, secrets, and the ocean's depths. M is the thirteenth letter of the alphabet and means the words "cooked" and "cook" in another language. M represents resurrection, rebirth, willpower, and sensitivity. You are not afraid to work hard and are organized. It likes to use its hands and is patient. The letter M is also represented by the number 4, as shown in the number of lines with which the letter is made up, which denotes the element of earth.

When the letter M appears in a person's birth name, it represents their power to regenerate and reinvent themselves due to past hardships or trauma. The letter M represents the 3 of Wands card in the tarot, representing ambition.

N

N loves to move and is imaginative and ambitious. When the letter N appears in a person's name, it signifies a person born during the new moon or at night. N is associated with the moon and the dark moon phase, which signifies rebirth and a new beginning. The letter N also applies the root number 5, showing duality and balance.

The letter N represents a birth closer to the earth, and as it is the eleventh letter of the alphabet, this letter represents water energy. The letter N represents the Ace of Wands card in the tarot, representing "a new beginning. "

O

O is pronounced with the lips completely, symbolizing supportive romance and love. O stands for water energy, while the circle is a Karmic symbol for completeness. It also represents the moon, which often signifies that words that use the letter O contain the words "moon" or "me." O is associated with endings and beginnings, death and rebirth. Being the 15th letter of the Pythagorean alphabet, O means the word "omega" in another language. O represents a queen and is linked with feminine energy and intuition. The root number 6 also applies to this letter,

When the letter O is on your name, it represents someone who loves to travel and explore. The letter O represents the Knight of Cups card in the tarot, which symbolizes the knight traveling through a beautiful place.

P

P stands for the element of earth in the tarot card, the 2 of Coins, which are two coins held together to represent wealth and prosperity. P is the sixteenth letter of the alphabet and stands for the word "penis." It symbolizes the element of earth in the tarot card, the 5 of Pentacles, " a woman who is intent on her material goals and financial and physical security. Relating to the root number 7, you tend to be spiritual and passionate in your life path, but sometimes you are too idealistic and may be too stubborn in your ways.

The letter P represents someone who focuses their energy on achieving a goal and is not afraid to work hard or take risks.

Q

Q is pronounced with the lips slightly open, representing silence, secrets, and the ocean's depths. Q is the 17th letter of the alphabet and stands for the word "quiet. " Q represents resurrection, rebirth, willpower, and sensitivity. You are not afraid to work hard and are organized. It likes to use its hands and is patient.

When the letter Q is initiated in a person's name, it signifies that the person has a quiet strength. It could also signify that this person was born at night or close to the time of the new moon. The letter Q represents water energy in the tarot cards, the 5 and 6 of Cups.

R

The letter R has a short stem with two lines and is not pronounced with the lips completely or completely closed, symbolizing silence, secrets, and the ocean's depths. R is the eighteenth letter of the alphabet and stands for the word "resurrection. " This letter is represented by the root number 8, where things tend to be in extremes.

The letter R represents resurrection, rebirth, willpower, and sensitivity. You are not afraid to work hard and are organized.

S

S can indicate changing directions in the middle of a project or plan and needs to guard against too many changes. S is the sixteenth letter of the alphabet and stands for the word "sex. " When the letter S appears in a person's birth name, it indicates a person who is very determined and focused in their efforts of achieving a goal and getting their point across. The root number 9 applies to the 18th letter, appealing to the humanitarian side of your soul.

The letter S represents fire energy in the tarot card, the 8 of Wands, which represents burning anger and someone impatient.

T

T is a peacemaker and peacekeeper who must balance sharing the Truth, even if it means temporary disharmony to trust that you will need to revisit peace. T is the seventeenth letter of the alphabet and stands for the word "truth" in the word "truthfulness. " This letter also applies to the root number 1, where things are perfect in their beginning and end. It is commonly associated with intelligence, logic, and the spoken word.

When the letter T is included in a person's name indicates that that person is honest by nature and may live by spiritual beliefs. T represents air energy in the tarot card, and the 10 of Swords represents a conflict or disharmony in relationships.

U

U is pronounced with the lips slightly open, representing silence, secrets, and the ocean's depths. This letter has various pronunciations depending on the language. U is the fourteenth letter of the alphabet and stands for the word "underwear. U" U represents resurrection, rebirth, willpower, and sensitivity. You are not afraid to work hard and are organized. The root number 2 also applies to this letter, representing the balance between two sides.

With the letter U, it indicates a person who is underestimated by others due to their shy nature or lack of assertiveness. The letter U represents fire energy in the tarot card and the 8 of Pentacles.

W

W represents a person stretching out two arms and a mountain range. It goes deep into the unconscious to gather resources for wisdom. W is the thirteenth letter of the alphabet and stands for the word "woman." The root number 3 applies here, too.

Letter W represents that this person has a very adventurous spirit and likes to travel to new places. The 6 of Wands in the tarot card also symbolize a young woman who travels the world with her friends to explore and discover new cultures.

X

X represents the number 24 and the single-digit 6 of human love. It can be open and ecstatic or lead astray by its sexual desires. X is the 25th letter of the alphabet and stands for "crossing out". This letter represents the root number 4 as well. It represents someone who does things on their terms while never compromising their integrity. The letter X represents the qualities of air and fire in one's soul. Additionally, it symbolizes transition and transformation.

When the letter X appears in a person's name, it represents that this person has a keen intellect, usually in scientific fields. It may also signify that this person lacks trust in others and is too stubborn in their ways. The letter X represents water energy in the tarot card, and the 9 of Cups, which represents a cup filled with something sweet and pleasant.

Y

Y is pronounced with slightly open lips, representing silence, secrets, and the ocean's depths. Y is the twenty-fifth letter of the alphabet and stands for "gypsum". This letter represents the root number 5 as well. It contains the energy of both life and death and wisdom.

The letter Y represents fire energy in the tarot card, and the 9 of Pentacles represents someone knowledgeable and upholds "old money" values.

Z

Z is pronounced with slightly open lips, representing silence, secrets, and the ocean's depths. Z is the twenty-third letter of the alphabet and stands for "zirconium". This letter represents the root number 6, which contains the energy of both empathy and compassion.

When the letter Z appears in the birth name, it indicates that this person is independent and that their mind is capable of great intellectual pursuits. The letter Z represents water energy in the tarot card, the 3 of Cups, which shows where you could restore peace.

Chapter 7: The Code Behind Your Astrology Number

The celestial bodies carry frequencies that can be used to divine our soul code, and these frequencies can inspire us to own the magic within us and manifest our dreams. When we apply numerology to the position of the stars and planets at the time of our birth, we uncover more layers and deeper understanding.

How to Interpret the Numbers in your Birth Chart

The only number you need to pay attention to in the longitude column is the first number with a degree symbol; this is the ascendant. This number is the first phase of your life - like Aries being the first sign in the zodiac. This number generally represents your life purpose or role in the world you were born to fulfill. You will often instinctively know what planet represents this energy.

The Longitude column shows a 360° cycle and goes through each sign for one year, starting and ending at your birth sign. For example, if you are born on July 4, you will join the sign of Cancer, which ends on July 22, then enter the sign of Leo from July 23 until August 22.

You'll see the Aries icon next to the Sun if you know your astrology symbols. Highlight or write out all the numbers you see in the longitude column of the planet table.

The houses are the same as the planets, but the degrees differ. Each house represents a 30° segment of the zodiac, so all the planets in the longitude column will have a corresponding number in the house column.

The Houses

House placements are explained in your natal chart as Ascendant, Point of in your natal chart, Midheaven, and Inclination. These four placements give you an idea of the planet's house position, and the house symbol usually appears above the house number. Say your Sun is in Aries in the longitude column, and your houses are in the eleventh; this means your Sun will be roughly between 0° and 30° in the zodiac's eleventh house.

Some sources say the Ascendant rules anything in the First House, with planets elsewhere falling under the orb. At the same time, some give the Ascendant a more passive role, delegating the role of ruling the First House to planets in a house that rules the same sign as the Ascendant. You can arrive at a more precise house placement by calculating the planet's degree house and hour house with the help of an app or website dedicated to planetary transits.

The Planets

Planetary positioning is vital information in your birth chart, as it can indicate your innate talents, challenges, and gifts. Planets in the sign of the Ascendant represent what makes us unique as individuals. Other planets in the same sign signify our buds that haven't yet burst into full bloom. While you can use the major transits to bring you opportunities and insights, we can't do without them because we can spend an entire lifetime without them changing.

- **Sun:** denotes your inner light, identity, and creative life force. The Sun is your soul's purpose. It marks an individual's identity and the traits you share with others. Interesting - it is also the signifier for the highest position in an organization. It's the ruler of the First House and influences your personality, expression, and how you integrate into the world.

- **Moon:** aligned to your emotions, moods, instincts, feelings, and subconscious habits. The Moon is your emotional body. It is home to your intuition, mood swings, and the reality you perceive. It represents who you are at your most vulnerable and the areas of your life you should be most attuned to. You can uncover your natural emotional patterns by referring to your Moon's sign and house positions in your chart.

- **Mercury:** tells how you express yourself and communicate, using reason and analysis. Mercury is your mental body. It reveals how you process information and communicate in written and oral forms. It represents your ability to multitask, cognitive abilities, and reasoning skills. Mercury also governs your sense of humor. The planet rules the Third House and influences how you express your ideas, connect with others, and value.

- **Venus:** shows love, beauty, creativity, money, values, sentiments, your creativity, and what pleasures you. This planet aligns with your relationships, attraction, and values. It represents your physical desires, intimacy needs, and how you relate to yourself and others. It represents how you show love and affection towards yourself and others, and it is how you connect with other people. You will always attract people who are energetically in tune with your Venus placements and abundant currency amounts in line with placements in your money houses.

- **Mars:** your energy, libido, will, sexual desires, romantic attraction, and creative drive. Mars is the planet that represents your body and vitality. Mars represents your physicality and sexual vitality, your competitive drive, determination, and stamina. It reveals the areas you should emphasize to cultivate a more powerful physical presence. This planet will energize your career and daily interests. You will want to exercise your body and use your passion to fuel your drive for success.

- **Jupiter:** the largest planet, governs expansion, what brings you joy, gratitude, honor, wisdom, and tolerance. This planet shows your abundance, happiness, philosophy, guidance, public schools, leaders, charities, media, movie stars, famous people, and politicians. Jupiter rules optimism, greatness, growth, expansion, idealism, and religious influence. It also reveals where you overextend yourself financially or to worthily invest your time. It can reveal secret opportunities or career goals. It rules expansion, opportunity, and areas you should expand in your life and career.

- **Saturn:** your position in society and the laws that govern you. It shows your social rank. This planet represents your social standing and authority positions. It shows how you benefit from maintaining authority, authority positions, and known status in society. It shows the areas of life that may not be so easy for you - places where you may have to work harder than normal to conquer challenges and where you have to work harder to achieve your true potential. Saturn shows how it is beneficial to build your reputation through the work you produce and helps you overcome insecurity caused by fear of not being accepted.

- **Uranus:** shows your unique flare, how you adapt to sudden change, breakthroughs, exploration, and progressive ideas. As this is the planet of change, it governs rebellion, independence, technology, freedom, intelligence, innovation, leadership, modernity, and originality. Uranus rules new ideas, disruptive innovation, inventions, and the modern mind. It influences science, thought leaders, innovators, and trailblazers. It rules electronic devices and technology. It shows you your genius or ability to develop brilliant new ideas, inventions, or plans. It shows your individuality, independent streak, and ability to be ahead of your time.

- **Neptune:** your imagination, capacity for compassion and unconditional love, psychic gifts, and sensitivity. This planet is associated with your emotional body. It represents how you process emotions in the subconscious. It shows how you manifest dreams through creative expression, raise your consciousness through belief in a higher power or connection to a cause larger than yourself, connect with a higher power or purpose through unconditional loving compassion, and use your natural intuitive gifts. It indicates how you channel energy and consciousness to achieve your higher purpose or certain psychological goals. It governs your sense of compassion, empathy, selflessness, and love and will help you move others through unconditional love. It also reveals your innate psychic abilities, extraordinary talents, open-mindedness, and unconscious motivations. People with strong Neptune

- **Pluto:** your source of power, position, capacity to transform, sexual desires, deepest hopes, and fears. This planet is associated with your body. It shows how you process power in your relationships and career. It indicates how you will benefit from gaining more power and what ends you will accomplish through your power. It reveals your ability to copy or absorb others' power. It also reveals your understanding of the subtle energies that may influence your future outcomes, your conscious and subconscious desires and passions, and how you process sexual energy with a passion for your work or audience.

- **Chiron:** your charisma, how you heal, your health, fertility, romantic instinct, emotional ties, secret wisdom. Chiron is not a planet, but it can help you understand how to connect with other people through your natural compassion. It has always been associated with healing since ancient times, and instead of indicating a wound, it indicates how you can heal others through compassion. Chiron represents your compassion for others, how you experience fulfillment through giving and receiving help, and your natural healing gifts. It shows where you seek comfort in professional development or career challenges, how you are personally connected to a new idea or goal that motivates you to achieve your goals, and how you benefit from helping others heal. It reveals hidden secrets you may have about others. Chiron can help you understand your past and prevent emotional attachments in the future.

It's best to know the degree symbol for house positions and the planet symbol in case a duplicate or order does matter. You'll know what they mean when you understand what the numbers represent with the help of your intuition and astrological knowledge.

Repeated Degree Numbers

You are now beginning to make important connections. Your astrology birth chart is widening the scope of who you are at a soul level and revealing hidden gifts you didn't know you had. Using the chart as a guide, you can find the most compatible and safe relationships for you. Take each number in your longitude column and write it down next to the house representing that number. Suppose you see the same name several times, circle or highlight that number. This will help you to see more clearly. For example, if the planet Uranus repeats twice, that tells you quite a lot about this part of your life from where your soul was before you came into this lifetime. Uranus is about breaking free from the normal constraints of society to pursue your genuine self.

Repeating degree numbers in your birth chart means that you will repeat various aspects of your life in cycles until you learn the lessons of those experiences. They may also indicate that life will show up in unexpected ways to explore residual issues and unfinished business from previous lifetimes. What you might repeat most strongly in life are lessons you've failed to learn or need to work on again. This will often result in overcoming failure and success simultaneously and learning to manage life and relationships in a balanced manner.

You will also notice a rising or falling pattern in your astrology birth chart. Rising repeats the number in the longitude column going up to the 12th house. The 12th house indicates endings, major life changes, and feeling out of harmony with yourself. If you have repeating numbers up to 12, this shows that major endings and major changes will occur until you learn to manage that part of your life properly.

A major life lesson is to overcome any doubts about who you are and what you wish to pursue in life. When you repeat the number, this tells you to ground that energy into your reality. It will manifest in inevitable ways. Your true life path often starts with doubt. You must test the waters out for yourself and become more confident by tying your belief in yourself to your actions. Repeating numbers suggest you have reached the point where you can be confident in yourself and have faith in yourself.

A repeating degree applies to a specific part of your chart. If you repeat the degree number going back ten years from today, all the houses will position themselves similarly. You may notice some elements remain the same while others will repeat or cycle in other ways. These subtle changes help you make different life choices based on the path of least resistance by guiding you to a repeating degree number you haven't yet experienced.

Live your life without restrictions, and discard self-judgment. Be aligned with the Divine Plan by trusting everything is working out for the best. Turn to the glory that is you, revealed in your true soul code.

Chapter 8: Your Personal Cycles

A continuous series of Personal Cycles is started that measure and describe the active energies influencing your life. This cycle can intensify your energy and bring you closer to your higher self and its energy. Personal Cycles track your life on an ongoing basis so that when you explore life, they can speak to you intimately and gradually unlock their mysteries through your personal cycles.

The Essential Numbers in your Personal Cycle

Your Personal Cycle is how your energies create your reality as you exist in the physical realm. A simple explanation: you draw the line of your personal energy from you through the active energies you use to create your life. These energies form your personal cycle, encircling you like a circle of white light. For each of us, these energies are different but "normal" because these energies guide everything from your birth to growing up.

These points become significant when you understand where they are right now. Understanding this information, you can begin to alter your life in ways that bring you greater joy, love, pride, prosperity, and opportunity.

The beginning of your personal cycle begins at birth. Often, these cycles are like the beginning of your week. Yet, your birth is much more significant. It represents your starting point in your current lifetime. This is where you begin anew and realize you have free will and everything is possible for you. This energy that guides you throughout your life becomes blocked or has too much abundance and begins to spin out of control. Your current life cycle consists of the following:

- **Your Personal Year:** This is the energy you feel on the day of your birth. This position is constant every year and represents your basic energy.

- **Your Personal Month:** This is your energy vibrating each month differently. Every day is influenced by the energy of the day and the month you were born, adding to these energies each month.

- **Your Personal Day:** This is the daily energy that your body feels around you. This can feel like thoughts are running through your head at times.

Calculating your Personal Years

Your Personal Year vibration begins on your birthday, not on January 1. The shift we feel on New Year's Day is related to the Universal Year Number changing, not our individual Personal Year. Our Personal Years are important because they indicate how strongly our energy influences our life. For example, if your Personal Year vibrations are high, you will feel a strong drive to succeed. While this drives some people to great accomplishments, others may feel pressured to complete certain goals, or they will crave certain items. This energy will manifest in different ways depending on the quantity of your Personal Year energy and how you allow yourself to use it.

Realize that how you view the world and your goals determine how you will feel this energy. In general, high personal year vibrations are considered excellent. The greater your personal year vibration, the more likely your Personal Year represents how your personal energy pattern will unfold over time, which starts from the month you were born.

For example, your birthday is on February 19, 2018 which represents 2 + 1 + 9 + 2 + 0 + 1 + 8 in your root number sequence, ending with a compound number 23. When 2 and 3 are summed up, the root number equals 5. This is, then, your Personal Year number.

Your Personal Year starts in February and ends in January of the following year. Your energy may surge during your birth month as you start your new life cycle. You may also feel energy strengthen from the start of your birth month and continue throughout the next twelve months as you approach your following Personal Year.

Calculating your Personal Months

Your Personal Months change at the beginning of each month. To find your Personal Month number, add the number of the month in question to your single-digit Personal Year number for each month. This adds your personal year number to the number of your birthday for each month.

Using the example above, here is how it looks:

- For the month of April, which is equivalent to the number 4, add your Personal Year number, in this case, 5.

- In the equation, 4 + 5 = 9.

April is the fourth month of the year, and thus your Personal Month number is 9. Personal Month numbers can change from month to month depending on personal birthdays and other external influences that impact your personal energy.

Calculating your Personal Days

Using the previous example, take your Personal Month number and add it to a specific day you prefer. For instance, your Personal Month number in our example and today is the 31st:

- This equates to 9 + 3 + 0 = 13.

- Since this is a compound number, you must add 1 and 3, to which the answer is 4. This is now your Personal Day number.

You can read the descriptions of the Personal Day and Personal Month numbers in the next chapter.

Your Personal Cycles

When a Personal Cycle number aligns with one of your Three Important Birth Numbers, you will experience profound growth and more opportunities. One of the best ways to understand this process is by understanding your Personal Day, Month, and Year numbers to guide you in empowering your life and serve as your rudder for your journey lifeboat. Your Personal Cycle, which powers up when it aligns with your Destiny Number. Like the energy of a solar or lunar eclipse, you can experience changes in your life that are unlike anything you have ever felt before.

Remember that your Personal Cycle helps you create realities, events, and experiences through active energies, the vibrations of energy you create in your life. Like an artist's masterpiece, each detail has meaning and represents important lessons for you to integrate into your being.

If your Personal Year and Personal Month activate one of your Important Birth Numbers, you will have triple intensification Power Cycle days. Take advantage of any Power Cycle activation to intensify your vibrations and initiate new and profound changes in your life.

Chapter 9: Personal Cycle Meanings

Every nine years, you begin a new 9-year cycle every nine years. Any time your 9-year cycle ends on your 9th, 18th, 27th, or others, or begins again on the 10th, 19th, 28th, or succeeding ones, you may feel a major change in your life. This is the best time to release and unburden your soul from past burdens and begin anew. Reflections are a good time of the year to renew commitments and promises you may have made to yourself or made during previous endings and beginnings of the nine-year cycle.

You have an idea of how you should live. Your life is an opportunity to demonstrate your ideals about how to live. This month expresses your commitment and dedication to living your life according to your philosophy. When cycles are right, you are in sync. You flow with life's cycles instead of resisting them. When you flow with life's cycles, you are not at the mercy of life's dramas. You arrive less frazzled and burdened and with the know-how to deal with them effectively when they arise.

When your Personal Year, Month, or Day Number matches with any of your Root or Destiny Numbers, the energies work for you, helping you in your endeavors to bring the ideal in your soul to fruition. If you encounter difficulties, you must act to realize the ideal. You can not attract your ideals or expect ideal adjustments to your life if you do not take concrete steps to make it real in your life.

Reflect on the personal values and beliefs you have discovered from which you choose to act in your life. You have unique skills to bring you closer to this realization. When life's dramas shift you off course, be aware of this and use your discernment to resolve them. Resolve them at the root level by addressing what needs to shift within you to bring about the changes in your life. Keep making adjustments and direct your energies at the vital centers, or chakras, to bring your intentions to fruition.

Personal Cycle Number 1

The Personal Cycle Number 1 represents new beginnings, fresh ideas, and enthusiasm for new experiences. It is a time for passion, vitality, action, leadership, and accomplishments. The only true regret you may have is the utter lack of time to accomplish all you would have liked. This cycle heightens your sensitivity to energies and forces around you and enables you to see change when it occurs. It is a cycle to take stock of what you have accomplished, what elements of your life need renewed commitment or must be shifted, and make adjustments to align your flow with this cycle. Each number in this cycle shows a particular aspect that this year can bring for you.

You have an idea about what is possible. The Personal Cycle Number 1 represents your idealism, which has persisted for many years. Now is the time for you to bring this idealism to fruition. You have a vision of a better future. Because you have put in the hard work to make your present life a reality, now is the time to choose how you want to continue your life in the upcoming year. Your dreams are no longer ideological fantasies. They result from pursuing an ideal that has long been in your soul. There is a strong need to purge the past so that you can live in the present.

This cycle requests that you reinvigorate your commitment to the ideal in your soul. You have absorbed many influences along the way that have interfered with your realization of your ideal. Today is the day to start anew and cleanse your aura with an energy of possibility and renewal. This opportunity is great for your inner power. Use it to overcome limitations that keep you from creating your ideal life. Move beyond your potential obstacles by acting with power. Do what is necessary to fulfill your ideals.

Personal Cycle Number 2

The Personal Cycle Number 2 appeals to creativity, cooperation, balance, and harmony. Your greatest commitment should be to balance your career and personal life and a harmonious relationship at home. You may find that one or both of these areas demand more of your attention and energy than you desire. Your relationship may be out of balance. Perhaps your partner wants more of your time than you can give, or your relationship needs more love; your career may also require more attention than you feel able to give. With your productivity is your sense of harmony with others. Conflicting commitments, intimate relationships, or a business partnership may place added demands on you in the coming year, which throws you off balance.

A partnership is a source of your life's support, strength, and creativity. This year will bring more opportunities to experience greater support, strength, and creativity through partnerships. Allow yourself to become open to what you may discover as a partnership source of support in your life. The theme for this year is about partnerships and relationships in general, and partnerships where both people hold many of the roles and responsibilities in life.

You may resist cooperating because you long to be your boss or fear that the Universe will control you in a relationship. The desire to compete and control others may arise in you and threaten the partnership. If you are the controlling type, it may be easier for you than you think to become a partner that goes off on his own. The competition and desire to control others may become a way to separate yourself from a relationship that is not working effectively. You may also react to frustrating relationships by resisting the need for cooperation or a need to compromise.

Personal Cycle Number 3

The Personal Cycle Number 3 is a period of excitement, creativity, happiness, laughter, and learning. It also represents a time of social involvement and personal fulfillment. It is known as the witty cycle because of the potential for amusing remarks and quick-witted responses. However, this short-lived part of your life brings little in the way of solid accomplishments.

Laughter and imitation often overpower your authentic self-expression and genuine feelings toward others. Sometimes you shine brightly but may confuse this with a shallow sense of self-importance and egotism. Too much of this cycle's energy may result in a lack of respect for yourself and those around you, jeopardizing your friendships and relationships. It can also lower your self-esteem and dampen your creative talents. This cycle is a time to let go of pretenses and your idealization of others and develop authentic relationships with others.

This cycle produces an exceptional love of learning. You are hungry for information yet know how to retain such information for later use. You are open to receiving information with ease. Use this knowledge effectively in the future. There is a strong desire to be the party's life, have fun, and experience all the positive things in life. This year, you may find yourself more involved with social events than with your professional pursuits. Pay attention to your friendships, relationships, and family ties that enhance and encourage your independence and sense of self-fulfillment.

Your self-expression, your creativity, and your relationships with others are called upon this year. There are social and creative opportunities available to you this year. Celebrate your uniqueness and your true feelings now. Express yourself openly and acquire the support you need from others. This year, personal energy, self-expression, and creative fulfillment support your happiness and growth. Allow yourself to have fun and be playful. If you desire improvement through creativity, you will find that this applies primarily to the material side of life this year. If you are an artist or musician, a novelist or playwright, you will enjoy popularity and prosperity this year.

Personal Cycle Number 4

Personal Cycle Number 4 represents patience, self-restraint, rationality, organization, and practicality. It represents break through, determination and materiality, as well as hope for stability in your life. If you are familiar with this cycle, you may have noticed that this is the first time the number 4 has come around for you in a long time. The number 4 brings self-restraint and contributes to personal maturity, but causes you to question yourself. You may struggle with your stability and your beliefs. You may question your beliefs' reality, making expressing your own point of view difficult. Furthermore, you may hold back your words and ideas in the coming year to avoid confrontation or conflict. You may have difficulty staying focused on what is important in your life. You may seek stability through conventional methods of organization. Sometimes it is easier to go along with the majority than to believe what you believe.

When Personal Cycle 4 comes around, you tend to complain or criticize everything. This year, your cycle may challenge those beliefs and lead you to question them. This cycle brings about new challenges and changes of its own. Personal Cycle Number 4 asks you to consider what you believe and why you are the way you are. You need to examine your situation closely and let go of unfounded beliefs and beliefs that did not serve you well in the past.

The number 4 inspires you to take a holistic view of your situation. The personal cycle number 4 brings courage and strength. It is associated with the color yellow and the organ of the stomach. This cycle encourages organization and practicality in all you do. It also promotes a spiritual approach to life and emphasizes the need for attentiveness and tolerance. Your organizational skills and sincere quest for stability serve you well this year.

Personal Cycle Number 5

Personal Cycle Number 5 is associated with the desire for freedom, adventure, risk, and surprises. It is a time to enjoy yourself and appreciate others. It is a time when you tend to be outgoing and comfortable with change. If you are unfamiliar with the number 5, you will notice that this year is a stage of culmination and transition in your life. You may change jobs, change professions, leave a relationship, or move across the country, leaving you in nothing but a white void. You may feel like you are in a white void, but much is available this year if you remain open to possibilities.

Personal Cycle Number 5 is a part of change and transformation. It is not a time of concrete achievements but aspirations and opportunities to make significant new beginnings. You are learning to trust your intuition this year and your ability to make changes. If you do not trust your intuition, making decisions and changing a habit or an unsatisfactory relationship may be hard. This number is a state of tolerance and tolerance for others, accepting their beliefs and attitudes. It is an accepting attitude that allows you to share your increasing independence. The personal cycle number 5 is an episode of freedom and exploration and demands tolerance for others. Accept the things you cannot change. Let the rest go and let others be. Your desire for freedom may lead you out of your routine or out of a relationship that no longer serves you. Your rebellious side emerges when you venture into the unknown or challenge convention. Your thoughts and behavior show daring, originality, and resourcefulness. You may make new friends or have a new romance this year.

Personal Cycle Number 5 is a period of happiness, freedom, and enjoyment. You have a zest for life and a willingness to step out of the four walls of your cocoon to take risks. You are willing to change, take risks, and step out of your routine. This cycle encourages you to develop your intuition and trust your instincts. If you are open to possibilities, this year provides a wealth of chances for success in all areas of life.

Personal Cycle Number 6

Personal Cycle Number 6 deals with relationships, taking on responsibilities, and the need to be dependable in everything you do. It challenges you to be committed in all areas of your relationship, business, and personal life. These commitments may stretch you to your limits this year. If you are familiar with the number 6, you may remember that this cycle marks the end of the previous cycle. You finish what is started and become aware that your life is balanced but needs to be purified and cleansed from time to time.

You may take on responsibilities for your partner, family, or friends this year. Family partnerships and business relationships strengthen as others recognize your reliability and dependability. If you are in a relationship or partnership, you may feel limited in the scope of activities in which you can be involved. Your emotional needs are important but need to be balanced with the needs of others with whom you are involved.

You may sense that romantic opportunities are available but may be intimidating or challenging. If you stay in a relationship, you may feel a need to shake up or break from it. Both single and married individuals may find their relationships expanding. If you are single, you may feel more involved with your partner's business affairs, and there may be opportunities to travel together. You may take on some additional responsibility at work. If you are married, you may discover that your spouse takes on more responsibilities at home and work. The number 6, is all about service to others. You may find yourself putting others ahead of yourself. You may also find yourself juggling many responsibilities at once. Balancing the emotional needs of others with your personal needs becomes important.

Personal Cycle Number 6 is a point of sacrifice, self-restraint, and a chance to examine your beliefs and relationships. You need to devote your energy to others' needs rather than your own this year. This part of your life is a year when you can find yourself wanting to please others to the point that your talents and abilities are neglected. You may neglect your innate needs if you do not consider your own needs. It is important to pay attention to your emotional needs this year. You have heightened sensitivity, so you must learn how to balance your goals with the needs of those to whom you devote yourself.

Personal Cycle Number 6 represents selflessness, service, and a desire to help others. You have sensitivity, which you can turn to personal advantage if you learn how to balance your needs with those of others.

Personal Cycle Number 7

Personal Cycle Number 7 is usually a period of spiritual reflection and contemplation. It is a phase where self-examination and a spiritual healing process in which you realize that others' opinions or points of view are more valid than yours. You tend to detach from situations rather than deal with people and yourself. This year, you concentrate on yourself, your beliefs, and your life, becoming more aware of your spiritual self and thoughts. Personal Cycle Number 7 is a chance for inner growth and spiritual development and a time for meditation, prayer, stillness, and meditation. It is a time for you might turn to religion or spirituality to find security and comfort. There is often a lot of introspection this year.

You may find a new level of serenity and peace as you come to terms with new ideas, concepts, and relationships. You tend to be introspective and spend a lot of time alone. You withdraw from situations that you dislike and often isolate yourself from others. You may spend a great deal of time alone or in your world, thinking about yourself and your life. You may start a new job or try a new career. You may pursue North or initiate a new interest or hobby. You may begin correspondence courses or take college courses. You may take a trip to explore the world and yourself. This cycle brings challenges and changes, so you may experience frustration or difficulties this year. You may experience roadblocks in your job or your relationships as you deal with your need to constantly define what is right and wrong or good and bad for you. You may find yourself questioning your values or beliefs. You may find that you turn to religion and spiritual beliefs for answers.

Spiritual development is important if you so desire. As a reflective person, you understand the importance of balancing outer success and inner awareness. You can balance your need for social growth and interaction with the need for quiet time to reflect and contemplate. Personal Cycle Number 7 is a cycle time of introspection, reflection, and self-examination and a time to discover your spiritual self. You need to understand emotional issues to use them to develop your life and relationships with more understanding and compassion.

Personal Cycle Number 8

Personal Cycle Number 8 deals with money and financial gain and is a cycle of opportunities for you, particularly with your business career. Money is the literal oxygen for this cycle, which emphasizes your material needs and challenges you to fully use your intuitive and psychic sensitivities.

You strive to acquire prosperity, power, and control. It is a time for vigorous activity and excellent financial opportunities. If you use the qualities of this cycle wisely, you will find yourself in a position for a great financial windfall. If you are inspired by this cycle, you may find that you pursue your ambitions and accomplish your goals.

Money matters are prominent in this cycle so that you may feel wealthy and happy or find that you are constantly concerned about money. You may find yourself consumed by financial matters and constantly thinking of ways to make money. A windfall may come your way, or you may inherit money. You may earn a great amount of money, or you may become involved in a business partnership that is very good financially or may involve a windfall. You may find a girlfriend or boyfriend with great potential to increase your financial status, or you may inherit money or come into a lot of cash. This cycle's challenge is balancing your inner urge for accumulation with the need to give generously to yourself and others.

Personal Cycle Number 8 is for inner and outer prosperity and a time of financial gain. The opportunities afforded you this year can aid you in realizing your material dreams. You are inclined to use mystical and spiritual powers to manifest the good fortune you want in life and business. This lucrative and innovative cycle requires you to proceed cautiously during this time, particularly with legal and financial matters and contracts.

Your instincts are strong this year, so listen carefully to your intuition.

There may be hidden dangers or mistakes. Your psychic radar is sharp this year. Developing your intuitive abilities can help you gain the financial success you desire. You are inclined to pursue money and material things during this cycle.

Personal Cycle Number 9

Personal Cycle Number 9 deals with humanitarian ideals and a desire to serve humanity. It is a time of great development and transition, finding the balance you desire between the demands of your physical and spiritual life. Personal Cycle Number 9 deals with relationships and ways in which you can better solve your life problems. It is a year to develop emotional bonds with those who have important or special roles in your life. This year is particularly important for nurturing and protecting your relationships with family and friends.

The cycle's spiritual influence helps you to see life from a higher spiritual perspective. You have great inner resources and can release many negative feelings from the past and transform them into positive spiritual energy now available to you. It is a year to consolidate your personal growth so that you can be more aware of your needs and wants. If you are out of balance, you tend to feel cut off from others and isolated. This year is when you learn the art of balance, and this is the best time for spirituality, spiritual development, holistic health, and the pursuit of harmony between spirit and matter.

Spiritually, this cycle brings changes that lead to greater inner harmony. It is a time for spiritual pilgrimages and a quest for inner peace. It is a time to be introspective and seek the balance between the mind and the spirit within the universe. It is a time when you may use spiritualism to close the ending chapters of your life and prepare for the start of a new one. Perfectionism is a hallmark of this cycle. You may tend to be overly concerned with your feelings and needs. This cycle is about developing deeper spiritual feelings and beliefs. If you are unsure of your spiritual path, you tend to look outside the self for answers, which may cause you to wander at times during the year. This start is a year of growth and learning. The spiritual lessons you learn this year can be invaluable to you.

Spiritual Year Cycle Number 9 fosters learning and spiritual growth, insight, development, and self-exploration. It is a year when you become more aware of your feelings and the needs of others, particularly your feelings toward those closest to you. The spiritual lessons you understand this year can be important as you travel through this cycle, for you may become involved in face-to-face, group, or spiritual healing. You may also be involved in self-help and personal development classes that may help you become the person you want to be.

Chapter 10: Numbers and Your Connection to Inner Power

In chapters 3, 4, and 5, you discovered the detailed meanings of all single-digit and double-digit numbers. These three chapters are your ultimate guide to the numbers in your daily life.

Numerology allows us to explore our life's potential by emphasizing the numbers we encounter and the circumstances we are born into. It is a fascinating approach to life's puzzles. It does not answer every question, yet it gives us an intriguing glimpse into how we fit into the world. Finding out one's vibration number allows for a more profound understanding of how intense we are at certain points in our lives, who acts on our traits, and how we are perceived. It also helps us to discover which ideas or situations we tend to attract.

The vibrations of numbers are too high for people to hear them with their ears or even their eyes. The combination of the two sets creates audible frequencies that can activate any of the chakras. When someone contacts someone with a high vibration number, the results can be life-changing for the affected person. One's life path is the dominant vibration that characterizes an individual's characteristics. Each number vibration carries its energy and vibrations. Life path numbers are the most dominant vibration in the numerological chart of a person's life.

Number Callings

There may be times when you encounter numbers that come as repetitive numbers on your devices or when checking the time of your day, etc. Subtle helpers' impulses have charged or activated these numbers in your unconsciousness. These impulses come to your subconsciousness in the form of thoughts. When these impulses come into your subliminal levels, they go to the subconscious again; from there, they go to the conscious mind, which creates all thoughts, words, and actions. Therefore, all inner processes occur within the subconscious levels and not at the conscious levels.

Your conscious levels are only shells of your real self and are only used for receiving and transmitting outer stimuli and inner impulses to the subconscious levels for inner processing. Your subconscious mind handles all work, but your conscious mind is the carrier that carries the information from the subconscious to the conscious and aware levels. This book has given you a rudimentary understanding of the subconscious mind and the conscious levels. In this chapter, you will learn how numbers enter your subconscious mind and how to change these numbers based on your choices and decisions.

Time plays a very important role in the lives of people. Time affects human physical sensations such as hunger, physical thirst, satiety, fatigue, aggression, fear, and anger. Time also shows the seasons, the change of days and nights, and the periods of mammalian life, such as pregnancy, birth, periods of activity, and sleep.

You can connect with your soul by paying attention to the number of messages that come up for you several times a day. For instance, by looking at the time and noticing that it's 2:09 p.m, look at the overall message 2 + 0 + 9 = 11, which notes for

Master Number 11 signifying the balance between the seen and the unseen.

Your Residence Number

Address numbers affect your life differently, so it's important to know how your address affects you. Use these daily number reflections to help you find more balance, lightness, and clarity in your life. As you do so, notice and recognize any shifts that unfold.

You must calculate your building and unit numbers separately if you live in an apartment or condo. Given the spiritual meaning of the numbers 0-9 arranged according to numerology, together with a sound file for each number. The meanings are easy to remember because they are based on their names. The phonetic naming system is very easy to find the right sound for each number.

Calculating your Address Number

Computing your Address Number can lead you to understand yourself better. Your Address Number can bring into focus issues regarding family relationships, emotional issues, and hidden desires. Living with rented accommodation impacts your Address Number as well.

Some say that numbers have powers that affect random people even if they are not in contact with the persons affected. The believers in these numbers say that the numbers might come from spirit guides, guardian angels, or The Universe itself.

- Let's look at our first example: 123 Main Street. You can add the numbers on your address, like 1 + 2 + 3 = root number 6, taking your artistry and creativity to another level.

- On our second example: 27B Penny Boulevard. When there is a letter before the building, first take the digits to get 2 + 7 = 9. The numerical digit of B is the root number 2. In this case, you will have to add 9 and 2, getting the sum of 11, which is a Master Number that calls to a higher power.

Remedy for Address Number Challenges

You can add a secondary positive vibration to your home or office by placing a 3 inside the front door. In Feng Shui practice, the 3 in the Northwest corner activates the Wealth Area of your home. Whenever you add a new positive element to your home, you must move the number 1 or 9 away from you in the space. If it is behind the door, take the 1 or 9 out of the space by going into the Backyard or Garden area and placing an X sign across the door. If the door faces the Northwest, you must move it away from the Northwest corner. In the Southeast corner, rotate the 9 to the Southwest and close it.

In Chinese philosophies, certain numbers symbolize certain periods. Since life is constantly on the move, numbers that symbolize a period help determine the type of period that a person may experience, regardless of whether we are conscious of it or not. With Numerology, certain numbers can correct any challenges in the existing Destiny Numbers within a household. From this, you can better understand how numerical vibrations affect offspring within a house.

The numeric vibrations of these numbers can reveal a person's past and present life. Infinite numbers can reveal the days ahead in a person's life. The date you were born has the greatest impact on the numbers in your name, the date of your marriage, and the age of your children. If the date of your wedding is consecutive to your birthday, the number and your name, the sum of your birth dates, and the birthdates of the people you are close to, will affect your future and the future of your loved ones, including your children. Likewise, your birthday and the approximate ages of your children indicate the numerical vibrations in your family system. If your birthdate number conflicts with your Destiny Number, there will be a tendency towards emotional dependency, and you will have to be in a desperate search for love.

The individual number vibration affects your life decisions, both consciously and subconsciously. Indeed, numbers don't lie, so pay attention to the number of coincidences and repetitions that happen to you throughout the day. Changes in the numbers of your daily reflections may start happening when you focus on your number vibrations first. With the help of your numbers, you may start to notice their guidance and nudges as thoughts or inner impulses that come forward from the depths of your unconsciousness. Talking about yourself and having the opportunity to convey your thoughts, ideas, and feelings to another person positively affect your life's progress.

Chapter 11: Empower by Repetition

The spiritual code of your name signifies your unique vibration and magnetic energy. Your unique human energy vibrates at a specific frequency or energetic signature; this number establishes your place among other humans. Your spiritual energy may display several combinations of numbers that create a vibration or frequency. This frequency is the "signature" you project to the universe.

In Numerology, repetitive numbers and letters can magnify your divine energy. As you discover your life's purpose, paying attention to the messages of repeat numbers or letter combinations is important.

Repetitive Letters in your Name

Repeating letters in your name can positively affect your life. The bigger impact is made by repeating vowels because these vowels embody the qualities which you want to develop in yourself. What is important to notice when you have a repeating letter in your name is that the letter represents an ebb and flow of energy.

Another way letters are highly impactful in your name is by repeating initials. Every letter in a person's name has a specific vibration and meaning. Discovering the meaning of the letters of your name gives you a greater understanding of who you are. When you understand the importance of the letters in your name, you can manifest more of the qualities that are important to you. These repeating numbers in your name can give you insight into your life path.

The third method is based on the numbers in the Letter-Number Conversion table in Chapter 6. Using this table, check the number that most resonates with the letters of your name.

A, J, and S - Number 1

You must stay active to fulfill your goals. When you feel motivated in your project, you can exert endless energy with it. You can make decisions quickly. If you don't, you tend to feel out of sorts.

B, K, and T - Number 2

You cooperate well with others and provide a soothing, peaceful presence. You are popular and have a strong awareness of what's happening around you. You feel compassion and the ability to share ideas with others. You are highly sensitive and may go beyond your comfort zone to please others.

C, L, and U - Number 3

You are very artistic and creative, but you may scatter your creative energy by focusing on too many endeavors. Your natural curiosity and enthusiasm make you very persuasive and communicative. You communicate your ideas and issues easily with others. Watch overspending without regard to a set budget.

D, M, and V - Number 4

Time getting ready for a social occasion is a good time to focus on an achievement or goal that will allow you to keep your life flowing. When making a good impression, wear clothing and grooming carefully, and be proud of your possessions. You must work hard to grow your business and maintain control of it. You are a loyal friend and partner. You may need to show more aggression and assertiveness in your goals to bring balance to conflicting situations.

E, N, and W - Number 5

You are fun-loving, need freedom above all else, enjoy traveling and being in the media spotlight, and have an innate sense of humor. You also strive for a harmonious balance of rest and activity. Family is very important to you, but you must be careful with your emotional energy. You like providing comfort and reassurance to others.

F, O, and X - Number 6

You are devoted to family and love to nurture others. Your natural generosity and care make you an excellent counselor, and you may take on the responsibility of being your family's provider. You prefer stability in your environment and may be conservative in your choices. You are easygoing and outspoken, but sometimes you may feel guilty for being too much of a caretaker. You are sensitive to energy and aesthetics and feel best when your environment is beautiful and the relationships in your life are all harmonious.

G, P, and Y - Number 7

Concentration is important in understanding and remembering information. It is good for your health to engage in some form of meditation. You need to release tension through exercise, dancing, or movement. You are a very sensitive, intuitive person who must have quiet time for reflection. Your spiritual nature gives you an awareness of a higher power and an involvement with the mysteries of life. You strive to keep your life on a positive path and are determined to overcome obstacles toward the end of the day.

H, Q, and Z - Number 8

This intensification enhances your ability to analyze and research subjects with great depth and beyond boundaries. You may get too "into your head" and need alone time to process your tangential discoveries. Your intuition is strong, and you may use it to help others through medical or counseling work. Your analytical mind relies on your ability to discern patterns. You are protective of those you love and are dedicated to bringing a sense of purpose and peace to those around you.

I and R - Number 9

You are highly motivated to accomplish a body of work that brings you influence and financial security. You can work alone or in a group to achieve your goals. You help others attain their goals and are willing to create coalitions. Your intuitive nature helps you understand people quickly. You desire quality and will strive to secure the highest possible outcome. You are a humanitarian who can reach beyond personal love and activate universal compassion. However, you must guard against wanting to "save the world".

Missing Numbers in Your Name

In chapter 2, you learned how to assign each letter in your given birth name to a number. Sometimes, any number from 1 to 9 is missing from your name. When a letter is missing from the number assignation table, you have to look for it in the number conversion table for this number.

If you are missing a number in your name, discover the impact it may have on your life. Here are the missing numbers:

- **Missing Number 1:** Missing the 1 vibration indicates you must assert yourself, be courageous, and make your own decisions. You will experience a tendency to withdraw or ignore your needs in favor of others. Be courageous to keep your individual plan and be true to your beliefs. Confidence can help you reclaim self-esteem when your name misses the letters under the 1 vibration.

- **Missing Number 2:** Missing the 2 vibration indicates that you should practice cooperating with others and exhibit the utmost patience to proceed. Your ability to concentrate may motivate you to avoid responsibility because your job may be tedious and repetitive. In an awkward social situation, only say what is constructive and avoid avoidance.

- **Missing Number 3:** Missing the letters in number 3 vibration can indicate that you lack experience with fun and spontaneous creativity, adn probably underestimate yourself. Time spent focusing on various interests can help you develop your creativity more successfully. Artistic endeavors are a way to express your inner thoughts, values, and desires. Focus on staying positive and using your imagination without placing any boundaries.

- **Missing Number 4:** Missing the 4 vibration means you need to establish an organized and disciplined approach to your life. You need to acquire knowledge and increase your proficiency with practical problem-solving. Your strong emotions may be exaggerated and may affect your mind-body health. You may experience low energy with an unstable emotional balance. You may feel vague about your goals and have the desire to travel.

- **Missing Number 5:** Missing the 5 vibration is seldom found in Western names since the letters E or N are usually present. You need to learn to embrace change and adjust to new events in your path. Avoid becoming close-minded and confident in your direction. You are resourceful emotionally but may struggle with trust issues. Have patience and self-confidence to manifest your goals.

- **Missing Number 6:** Missing the number 6 letters may make committing to long-term relationships challenging. You may be more comfortable in social communities. You may consider taking on a teaching or counseling position. Missing the number 6 can mean being specific and clear about your direction. You need to provide stability in your environment to avoid destabilizing elements in your life. You may also need to take on extra family responsibilities.

- **Missing Number 7:** Missing the 7 code means you may not naturally want to look more deeply at issues or understand the "whys" and "hows" of life. You may avoid your spiritual nature and feel separated from your higher purpose. You may be highly aware of your verbal abilities and may be a leader others look to for clarity and wisdom. You may be less cautious than others and less prone to analyze.

- **Missing Number 8:** People missing the number 8 in their names are highly independent. They may attract people who challenge their enthusiasm, creativity, and courage. Conflict compelled you to develop and embrace your own beliefs. You often feel that others don't understand your single-minded and goal-oriented goals. You may experience restlessness and need to travel to follow your passions.

- **Missing Number 9:** Missing the number 9-related letters mean you are learning about human nature and have great potential to help others. You may be very loyal and committed to your direction, but you may neglect personal needs. You may tend to be impulsive and make emotional decisions out of desperation. Your strong intuition can help you decide others' thoughts and actions.

Images Behind the Alphabet

Each letter in the alphabet forms an image, and the shape of your initials reveals even more about your disposition and approach to life. It has a powerful, symbolic meaning that can influence your success and happiness. The numerical outline of your body describes the shapes of each letter. The letters can form straight, curved, or combined lines to express your purpose.

Straight-lined Letters

The letters A, E, F, H, I, K, L, M, N, T, V, W, X, Y, and Z are made of straight lines that indicate focusing on your plans. This focused energy helps you organize a purpose and gives you a sense of purpose in life. You understand the importance of getting it done and taking charge of your life. You are a loyal person who concerns yourself with ethics, quality, and safety. You will strive for success and accomplishment through planning and persistence.

Curved Letters

The letters C, O, S, and Q are made of curved lines that indicate flexibility and that you excel at adapting to circumstances. You led an active lifestyle growing up, and your flexibility helps you with ease and comfort. You may resist commitment or feel unfulfilled unless you are active in a creative or physical pursuit.

If not, you may desire a spiritual connection or abundance in your environment. You do well with social activities because you feel pure joy in them.

Combined Letters

The combined letters B, D, G, J, P, R, and U bring focus and flexibility. Combined letters can also mean you use your intellect to bring joy to yourself and others. Having a combination of the two provides you an edge in accepting both sides of situations.

These symbols mean you have many options; once you have determined the meaning of your letters, you can learn how to incorporate them into your plans for a successful career and life. As you learn numerology, you will begin to understand the meaning behind the number combination of your name. Analyze your name to guide your approach to activities and life choices.

The Law of Vibration

The Law of Vibration is the basis for all numerology and explains the value of your name and the numerological meaning assigned to each letter. Everything in the universe vibrates, and the law of vibration states that everything has its frequency. Every individual, place, or thing has a vibration or frequency. Everything from the smallest atom to the largest galaxy has its own vibration. You can measure the vibration by calculating its mathematical pattern.

The Law of Vibration describes the frequency of each letter in your name. The number and order of the vibrations in your name blend to create your life path number. This vibration is what draws your experiences and explains the lessons you learn from your experiences. Your challenge is to focus on your growth and aim for a higher purpose in life.

Your Family's DNA Numerology

You can notice this in families. There may be one number that many family members share, or a "family of numbers" appears over and over again, like 3-6-9, 2-4-8, 1-5-7, or any other combination. This spiritual code for your DNA numerology links a family member to others. When you share a family vibration, you are living in harmony with the energy of vibration and electromagnetic fields that affect your family members. If you're sharing a family vibration, you're likely well-adjusted, grounded, and generous. You are also likely to consider the needs of others. When you have a different vibration, it signals a slight departure from your family code. Your quest for a higher level of understanding about yourself will also guide you away from your family's vibration.

Each family member has a unique vibration reflected in their names, initials, or birthdates. Each family member has the opportunity to display their vibration powerfully. You may have lived a generation apart, but have the same vibration. You are also destined to influence each other and experience similar life circumstances. Furthermore, you may find yourself experiencing the same life challenges, but different emotional reactions. Your vibration may not change, but you may interpret the same events differently.

Chapter 12: Number Sequences

Number sequencing has been used worldwide since writing. It plays a big role in our society. For example, banks use number sequencing on every transaction to ensure that no one is trying to commit fraud or illegally withdraw money from the bank. They do this by having the person input the identification number first, followed by their password. If we were to make a mistake in inputting our identification, a bank worker would question us why we input the wrong number or series of numbers and ask them to repeat it.

Number sequencing was important to the ancient Babylonians, Chinese, Egyptians, and Mayans, who used number sequencing for different purposes. For example, the Mayans had many different number sequences and glyphs representing numbers. They had a variety of counting systems, adding machines, and calendars. The Babylonians had number sequences between 1 and 9 in base 60 with symbols for the numbers between 10 and 90. The biggest difference between these number sequences is that Maya had several glyphs that did not represent a specific number.

When the number sequences go downwards, you are pivoting in a new direction and changing course in some way due to letting go of a past idea, behavior, or decision. When you notice a repetition of any number, look up the meaning of the digit, and you'll get a clear message of how one area in your life is being intensified.

The 11:11 Portal

When the 11:11 portal appears, you may feel suspended in time, a wonderful floating sensation of momentary timelessness. It's a connection that is undeniable and hard to describe because it transcends our human mind. As your consciousness expands to encompass the Zero Point Field, you begin to feel yourself integrate this Light - this beingness - this consciousness. You begin to expand and "open" to the energies around you. You begin to experience these energies as yourself.

The double 11: 11 portal manifestation indicates that you are connected to the Zero Point Field and that Source consciousness is helping you fit into it. You start remembering who you truly are. You remember your Soul Self and your Divine nature as One with Source. This portal allows you to transcend the limitations of the mind and experience Source consciousness more powerfully. Now more than ever, we are being called to remember our True Self and to claim our Divine birthright. This portal is an invitation to remember and connect with the Higher Self, or the 'I AM' presence within.

When the triple 11: 11 portal appears, it is a time of great insight and accelerated spiritual growth. It is a time when your consciousness is profoundly expanded, and your sense of time is significantly altered. You will start to feel magnetically pulled towards more Light and more knowledge, as well as a connection to All That Is. I challenge you to embrace the Spirit, Truth, and Purity call. I challenge you to step into your power and embrace your Divine life purpose and mission. You are asked to expand your consciousness to include your Soul Self and Divine Power.

When you notice the number 11:11, you feel at one with the universe. The past and future are no longer important; you can experience life as it is meant to be experienced. Nothing changes your day as much as seeing this number sequence. Perhaps the repeating number sequence unlocks the door to higher consciousness, enabling you to see beyond the illusions of time and awaken to the surrounding energies. They see the pattern as sculpted gates swinging open to connect two realities. When an 11: 11 portal appears, you may want to express a certain thought or idea or do something to accomplish a certain goal.

When you witness 11:11, it is a spiritual wake-up call to embrace the unexpected. All inspiration comes from this unknown space, where worry does not exist. Once you've seen this number portal, you can't go back. The insights and illuminations you receive are lasting. When you see 11:11, you must leave everything behind and embrace the only constant: eternal life and timelessness. You unlock the gate for abundance as you relate to this number, and you can manifest using this spiritual time.

In the human experience, we need contrast to appreciate the diversity of life. We need to experience loneliness to appreciate oneness, sadness to appreciate joy, darkness to recognize light, war to choose peace, and aggression to feel the gift of kindness. To live in prosperity, you must align your internal and external worlds. Clear all your resistance and emotional debris, and you create room for the universe to bring you abundant gifts.

Time flies when you are engaged in an activity that fulfills you. Imagine if you could bring that quality to your everyday life. If you knew exactly what to do to fulfill your soul, you could spend your entire life doing things that make you happy. Wouldn't that be a great way to live? The numerology meanings of the number 1 are not very consistent, as they could range from very positive to very negative.

One is believed to be the number of man's primal state, fully reflecting his natural instinct integrated with the planet Earth.

The number 1 personality tends to be very spontaneous and has an outgoing and conquering attitude. Your personal world revolves around you, and you can go after what you want in life. One's natural instincts and drives are completely focused inwardly.

In these fast-paced and hectic times, it's easy to get out of sync, exhausted, and unfocused, and then it's easy to get ungrounded, untethered, and imbalanced. The numbers behind your existence can guide you in staying focused and centered. The empowering numbers, especially the 11: 11 portal, teach you that you create your reality; you have the power to manifest and create your destiny. They give you the tools you need to find your direction in life. The power of manifestation exists within all of us. Everything is energy and has a frequency, vibration, and pattern. Getting in tune and aligned with your vibration, your natural state, opens the door to abundance and allows you to manifest your reality and destiny.

Positive Affirmations – Part 1

Positive affirmations express the belief that a certain thing is possible. They can benefit anyone striving for a goal by teaching them to think positively. Some people read positive affirmations every day to achieve specific goals. You can benefit by repeating these simple statements to yourself to help you overcome negativity and succeed at your goals.

Repeating positive affirmations help you reach any goal you strive for by increasing your self-confidence, building a positive attitude, and boosting your determination. This helps you visualize your goal and realize the importance of reaching it. This can be any goal you have on your mind!

Affirmations can help you reach your goals faster as they are positive thinking. They involve repeating a phrase or statement until it becomes "second nature."

Now relax and calm down as you repeat each affirmation five times in a row for 2 minutes each. You will listen to the affirmation, and there will be a pause of 2 minutes after each affirmation to give you enough time to repeat the affirmation and let your brain process it.

I am open to learning about numerology and understanding its concepts.

I am confident in my ability to understand and interpret the messages of numerology.

I trust in the guidance I receive from numerology.

Numerology is a helpful tool that I can use to improve my life.

I am grateful for the guidance of numerology.

I use numerology to help me make decisions in my life.

Numerology is always accurate and reliable.

I always get what I need when I consult numerology.

I am thankful for the helpfulness of numerology.

I rely on numerology to help me navigate my life.

I am a powerful being, and I use my power to create my dreams.

I know that my dreams are a reflection of my highest self.

No matter what I dream, I always wake up feeling thankful for the experience.

I focus on having positive, beneficial dreams that help me in my waking life.

I allow my dreams to reveal themselves to me.

The world is my oyster, and my dreams are my pearl.

I am motivated and inspired by my dreams.

I am confident and secure in my dreams.

My dreams are a reflection of my soul's purpose.

I am living my soul's purpose, and my dreams reflect this.

I am grateful for my dreams and the guidance they provide.

I use my dreams to help me heal from my traumas.

I have forgiven myself for my mistakes, and I am now able to move forward in my dreams.

Nothing can stop me from dreaming.

I am powerful and in control of my dreams.

I absolutely love dreaming, and I am grateful for this amazing experience.

My dreams are a reflection of my highest self.

I am always connected to my higher self in my dreams.

I receive profound guidance from my higher self in my dreams.

In my dreams, I can go anywhere I want and be anyone I want to be.

I use my dreams to explore different aspects of myself.

I have regular lucid dreams that allow me to explore different aspects of my life.

I am fascinated by my dreams and enjoy learning about myself through them.

My focus is on having positive, beneficial dreams that help me in my waking life.

I am confident in my ability to dream and to control my dreams.

I know that my dreams are a powerful tool that I can use to improve my life.

I am inspired by my dreams and motivated to achieve my goals.

I am proactive in my dreams, and I make decisions that are in alignment with my highest good.

I receive guidance and support from the universe in all of my dreams.

Every experience I have in my dreams is another step in my journey toward creating the world I wish to live in.

With a positive and open mind, I am open and receptive to all the information I receive in my dreams.

I allow myself to be vulnerable in my dreams, knowing that I am protected.

I am excited to explore my dreams and to learn more about myself.

This is a beautiful world, and my dreams reflect the beauty of the world.

I am blessed with the ability to dream, and I cherish this gift.

No matter what numbers I see, they all mean something positive.

All numbers are vibrations that offer me insight and guidance.

Numerology is a tool that I can use to improve my life.

The numbers in my life are always working in my favor.

I am open to understanding the messages that the universe is sending me through numerology.

I am willing to learn about the meanings of numbers so I can interpret them correctly.

I trust in the guidance that I receive from the universe.

I know that the universe is always working in my favor.

I am grateful for the abundance of information that is available to me about numerology.

I am excited to learn more about this ancient wisdom so I can apply it to my life.

I am confident in my ability to interpret the messages that I receive from the universe.

I am open to receiving guidance from the universe through numerology.

I know that I am always aligned with my highest good.

I trust in my intuition to guide me to the meaning of the numbers in my life.

I am willing to put in the work to learn about numerology so I can apply it correctly in my life.

Positive Affirmations - Part 2

I know that I have all the resources I need to learn about numerology.

Numerology is one way for the universe y to communicate with me.

The messages I receive from the universe through numerology are always accurate.

I am always connected to my higher self, and I receive guidance from this connection.

I trust in myself and the guidance I receive from the universe.

I can use numerology as a tool for personal and spiritual growth.

Numerology is a helpful way for me to gain clarity about my life path.

No matter what numbers I see, they always have positive messages for me.

Numerology is an ancient wisdom that can help me improve my life.

I am open to learning about numerology and using it in my life.

I know that numerology is a safe and positive way for me to receive guidance from the universe.

I trust in the messages that I receive through numerology.

Numerology is always working in my favor.

The numbers in my life are always giving me positive guidance.

I am grateful for the guidance I receive from numerology.

I am confident in my ability to interpret the messages I receive through numerology.

I use numerology as a tool for personal and spiritual growth.

I know that numerology can help me understand myself and my life better.
I am open to the guidance that numerology has to offer me.
I trust in myself and the messages I receive through numerology.
I attract certain people and experiences into my life based on the vibrations of my birthdate.
My birthday is a special day that should be celebrated.
I am grateful for the day I was born.
I am grateful for the gifts and talents I have been given.
I use my talents to their fullest potential.
I am confident in myself and my abilities.
I attract good luck and fortune into my life.
I am open to receiving all the good that life has to offer me.
I live a charmed life.
I am grateful for my many blessings.
Everything I desire comes to me easily and effortlessly.
I am in alignment with my highest self.
My intuition is strong, and I trust it implicitly.
I live my life with purpose and meaning.
I make choices that are in alignment with my highest good.
The universe supports me in all of my endeavors.
My desires are quickly and easily manifested into reality.
I attract abundance in all areas of my life.
I am worthy of receiving all the good that life has to offer me.
I am grateful for my many gifts and talents.
I use my gifts and talents to their fullest potential.
I attract all the abundance I desire into my life.
Money comes easily and effortlessly to me.
I attract all the wealth and prosperity I desire.
I live in a world of abundance.
There is more than enough for me and everyone else.
My needs are always met, and I have more than enough to share with others.
I give freely of my time, energy, and resources.

I receive freely of others' time, energy, and resources.
We are all one, and we are all connected.
What benefits me also benefits those around me.
As I prosper, so do those around me.
I am generous and kind, and I receive the same in return.
I attract loving and supportive relationships into my life.
All of my relationships are based on love, mutual respect, and trust.
I am surrounded by love and light.
I am a powerful being, and I use my power to create the life of my dreams.
I am confident and secure in myself and my abilities.
I trust in myself and my intuition.
I am a powerful creator, and I create my reality.

Guided Meditation

Begin by lying down, letting yourself get comfortable, ideally flat on your back with your spine straight, legs uncrossed, arms at your side, palms facing open, however, if that is not comfortable for you, make comfort your priority and when you're ready, lovingly close your eyes.

Invite your awareness in words.

Tuning into your own inner landscape.

Feeling your breath.

Inviting it to flow as softly and naturally as it wishes.

Relaxing and allowing gravity to take over.

It's safe to let go.

To release into relaxation.

Now think about your intention for this practice.

Why do you want to connect with your higher self?

What is it that you hope to achieve?

Allow yourself to really feel into your intention.

And as you do, begin to see yourself in a dream.

It doesn't matter what the dream is about, simply that you are aware that you are dreaming.

And as you become aware that you are dreaming, you may begin to see the dream begin to change.

You have the power to change the dream.

You are in control.

And you may begin to fly, or to float, or to move in any way that you wish.

You may explore your dreamscape, or you may choose to simply relax and enjoy the experience.

Whatever you do, trust that you are safe, and that you are in control.

Begin to notice any feelings or sensations that you experience in the dream.

You may notice that you feel lighter than usual, or that you feel a sense of freedom and flexibility.

Allow yourself to explore these sensations, and to really feel into the experience.

Relax even more.

Feel your body.

It is light.

You are dreaming.

And as you become more aware of your dream, you may find that you can control it.

You may be able to fly, or to travel to different places.

Or you may simply choose to relax and enjoy the experience.

Whatever you do, trust that you are safe and that you are in control.

Trust what you are experiencing.

And begin to feel yourself merging with this imagery.

You see yourself as the dreamer and the dream.

And you may begin to feel almost a sense of blissful ease.

And nothingness at all, Almost.

You are able to control wherever the dream takes you.

And you may find that you can change the dream to whatever you wish.

You may choose to fly, or to travel to different places.

Or you may simply choose to relax and enjoy the experience.

You see people or creatures in your dream, and you know that they are a part of you.

You are safe.

You are in control.

You decide what happens in the dream.

You can clearly understand you are dreaming, and can take any action you want.

You can control what you see, where to go, what to do.

And when you are ready to come out of this practice, do so by first letting your awareness come back to where your body is right now.

Imagining roots anchoring you to the Earth, growing all along.

Either your back, in the back of your body, if you're lying down on your back, or whatever other part of your body is currently facing the Earth.

Just imagine, from your current angle, many roots are growing out of you.

And deep into the earth.

Allow yourself to imagine you are discharging any excess energy down, down through these roots, and letting that energy nurture the Earth as you only hold on to that which is for your highest, most loving good for now, to carry with you.

Moving forward and begin to really feel your body here now, noticing the points of contact between you and the surface on which you are resting.

And when you are ready, very slowly roll your shoulders, wiggle your fingers and your toes.

And only when you're ready.

Take your time as you open your eyes back to the world around you.

Thank you, namaste.

MELISSA GOMES

FREEBIES

AND

RELATED PRODUCTS

WORKBOOKS
AUDIOBOOKS
FREE BOOKS
REVIEW COPIES

HERE

HTTPS://SMARTPA.GE/MELISSAGOMES

Freebies!

I have a **special treat for you**! You can access exclusive bonuses I created specifically for my readers at the following link! The link will redirect you to a webpage containing all my books and bonuses for each book. Just select the book you have purchased and check the bonuses!

>> https://smartpa.ge/MelissaGomes<<

OR scan the QR Code with your phone's camera

Bonus 1: Free Workbook - Value 12.95$

This **workbook** will guide you with **specific questions** and give you all the space you need to write down the answers. Taking time for **self-reflection** is extremely valuable, especially when looking to develop new skills and **learn** new concepts. I highly suggest you *grab this complimentary workbook for yourself*, as it will help you gain clarity on your goals. Some authors like to sell the workbook, but I think giving it away for free is the perfect way to say **"thank you" to my readers**.

Bonus 2: Free Book - Value 12.95$

Grab a **free short book** with **22+ Techniques for Meditation**. The book will introduce you to a range of meditation practices you can use to help you develop your inner awareness, inner calm, and overall sense of well-being. You will also learn how to begin a meditation practice that works for you regardless of your schedule. These meditation techniques work for everyone, regardless of age or fitness level. Check it out at the link below!

Bonus 3: Free audiobook - Value 14.95$

If you love listening to audiobooks on the go or would enjoy a narration as you read along, I have great news for you. You can download the audiobook version of *my books* for **FREE** just by signing up for a FREE trial! You can find the audio versions of my books (depending on availability) at the following link.

Join my Review Team!

Are you an avid reader looking to have more insights into spirituality? Do you want to get free books in exchange for an honest review? You can do so by joining my Review Team! You will get priority access to my books before they are released. You only need to follow me on Booksprout, and you will get notified every time a new Review Copy is available for my latest release!

For all the Freebies, visit the following link:

>> https://smartpa.ge/MelissaGomes<<

OR scan the QR Code with your phone's camera

I'm here because of you

When you're supporting an independent author,
you're supporting a dream. Please leave
an honest review by scanning
the QR code below and clicking on the "Leave a Review" Button.

★★★★★

https://smartpa.ge/MelissaGomes

Printed in Great Britain
by Amazon